WEAL~~~
MANAGEMENT
MADE SIMPLE

Seven Simple—But Not Easy—
Lessons on Your Investments and Your Wealth

David B. Mandell, JD, MBA
Jason M. O'Dell, MS, CWM
Carole C. Foos, CPA

with contributions from
Robert Peelman, CFP®
Andrew Taylor, CFP®
Adam Braunscheidel, CFP®

Guardian
Publishing LLC
2017

Wealth Management Made Simple: Seven Simple—But Not Easy—Lessons on Your Investments and Your Wealth
David B. Mandell, JD, MBA; Jason M. O'Dell, MS, CWM; Carole Foos, CPA

© 2017 Guardian Publishing, LLC Tel: (877) 656-4362

ISBN: 978-0-9965569-1-0
Manufactured in the United States of America.

About The Authors

David B. Mandell, JD, MBA, is a principal of OJM Group, attorney, author, and renowned authority in the fields of risk management, asset protection and financial planning.

Mr. Mandell has co-authored the book *Wealth Protection: Build and Preserve your Financial Fortress* and *Wealth Secrets of the Affluent: Keys to Fortune Building and Asset Protection*, both published by John Wiley & Sons, the oldest book publisher in the U.S. and largest publisher of business books in the world. He writes regularly for numerous business periodicals and has been interviewed as an expert in such national media as Bloomberg and FOX-TV.

Mr. Mandell graduated with honors from Harvard University, with an A.B. in History. His law degree is from the UCLA School of Law, where he was awarded the American Jurisprudence Award for achievement in legal ethics. While at UCLA, he also earned an MBA from the Anderson School of Management. You can contact David at mandell@ojmgroup.com.

Jason M. O'Dell, MS, CWM, is a principal and managing partner of OJM Group. Mr. O'Dell is a co-author of eight books on his area of expertise. He has experience as an entrepreneur, financial consultant and investment advisor and has been working with high-net worth clients for more than 20 years.

Mr. O'Dell graduated with a Bachelor of Arts in Economics from The Ohio State University and has earned a Master of Science degree with an emphasis in financial planning. He serves on the Board of Directors of the Alzheimer's Association of Greater Cincinnati and is a member of the Financial Planning Association, Cincinnati Estate Planning Council and the Advisory Board of Partners Financial. You can contact Jason at odell@ojmgroup.com

Carole C. Foos, CPA, is a Principal of OJM Group, and a Certified Public Accountant (CPA) offering tax analysis and tax planning services to OJM Group clients. Ms. Foos has over 20 years of experience in public accounting in the field of taxation. She was formerly a manager in the tax department of a Big 4 firm and spent several years in public accounting at local firms. She has been a tax consultant to both individuals and businesses providing compliance and planning services over the course of her career. In addition to her work for OJM, Ms. Foos maintains a tax practice in Cincinnati.

Ms. Foos received a Bachelor of Science in Business Administration from Xavier University where she majored in accounting. You can contact Carole at carole@ojmgroup.com.

Contributing Authors

Bob Peelman, CFP®, is the Director of Wealth Advisors at OJM Group. He oversees the firm's investment advisory practice. He has over 14 years of experience in wealth management, where his career has focused on serving the needs of successful individuals, families, endowments, and foundations. Bob works with clients to help manage their wealth responsibly, grow it tax efficiently, and maintain it for years to come so that it fulfills the lifestyle they want to lead. Prior to joining OJM, Bob was a financial advisor with Morgan Stanley Wealth Management.

Bob received his Bachelor of Science in Business Administration from the University of Kentucky and has earned the designation of Certified Financial Planner™. You can contact Bob at bob@ojmgroup.com.

Andrew Taylor, CFP®, is a Wealth Advisor with over 20 years of experience working with affluent individual investors. His career in the financial industry has focused on providing customized investment management, and comprehensive wealth planning in a tax efficient manner for his clients. Prior to joining OJM Group, Andrew spent 13 years at Charles Schwab & Co. managing and growing a substantial practice in the greater Cincinnati area, and working with local attorneys and CPAs to implement integrated wealth planning for his clients. Andrew's experience also includes time as a Retirement Consultant at Fidelity Investments.

Andrew holds a Bachelor of Science in Business Administration from the University of Kentucky, is a Certified Financial Planner™ and a member of the Financial Planning Association. You can contact Andy at ataylor@ojmgroup.com.

Adam Braunscheidel, CFP®, is a Wealth Advisor at OJM Group. His responsibilities include account management, investment research, and comprehensive investment planning in a tax efficient manner for OJM clients.

Adam graduated from Xavier University with a Bachelor of Science in Business Administration. He has earned his Series 65 license and Bloomberg Equity Certification, and has earned the designation of Certified Financial Planner™. You can contact Adam at adam@ojmgroup.com.

Table of Contents

Everyone Starts Somewhere

"In the long run, it's not just how much money you make that will determine your future prosperity. It's how much of that money you put to work by saving it and investing it."
—Peter Lynch, American investor, philanthropist and mutual fund manager of the Magellan Fund at Fidelity.

Can You Answer the Following Questions?

How do I set financial goals for my family...or my business?

How can I plan for an uncertain and unpredictable future?

How do my investments fit into my overall financial plan?

Could I do more to reduce what I pay in taxes?

Have I done enough to protect my wealth while I built it?

 In our business, we speak with many clients and prospective clients every year. Regardless of their background, geographic location or even stage of career, they often have many of the same questions.

When we set out to write a book specifically on wealth management with information on planning and investing; we immediately began with the idea of creating a resource that could outline answers for the most common questions we hear from clients all the time. Virtually every question could be boiled down to the basic, underlying concern:

Am I okay now? Will I be okay in future?

We can't answer these two questions from a physical or mental perspective—but as it relates to money and finances, we will try. Money is not everything, but a recent American Psychological Association survey found that *money* is the leading cause of stress among Americans. Why are we all so stressed out about money? Because most of us are afraid that we will run out. No matter how much you have—it is a basic fear that you may lose all or a significant enough portion that would change your life for the worse.

We will attempt to answer many of your basic investing and wealth management planning questions in this book. However, the answers to these questions tend to lead to more specific questions about your *specific situation*, which is natural. When that happens, we will show you where to go next or simply how to get started. Everyone starts somewhere—and anyone can start with this book.

We are eager to share the knowledge we have gained from decades of serving individual investors and their families by focusing on what clients have asked us and found most valuable from our services.

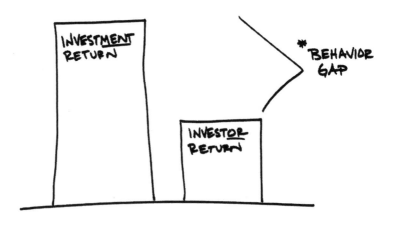

* LOOKS JUST LIKE IT DID 10 YEARS AGO.

© 2013 Behavior Gap

A major portion of this book will address the gap between how *investments* do—and how *investors* do. Carl Richards drew up this simple illustration over ten years ago to show this "Behavior Gap." Little has changed since he first drew this modest picture. We will explain in detail in the following Lessons—but for now simply note—in most cases we are our own worst enemies when it comes to our investing performance. We will show you why, but we want to start with what you will not find in this book.

What You Will Not Find Here

In the interests of saving your time and being fully transparent—we feel obligated to let you know what you will *not* find in this book.

This book makes no guarantees. We do not have a quick, easy, secret strategy. We do not offer get-rich-quick lessons or an easy path to financial freedom. There is no magic algorithm or fancy high-frequency trading, or other cutting edge technology promising to deliver high performance with zero risk.

If you pick only one piece of advice to take with you from reading this book—it should be: do not trust anyone who offers easy, get-rich-quick ideas. We will show you why these promises are always misleading and usually fraudulent.

Claims of easy money play on our psychology—we fall for far-fetched claims because deep inside we want them to be true. Of course, we want easy money, high performance with low risks—who wouldn't?

But there are no free lunches. Later sections of this book will describe how and why we fall for unrealistic promises; and we will provide additional information on what specifically to look for when scouting potentially fraudulent investments.

What You Will Find Here

 What we offer is a time-tested approach to wealth management, planning and investing that will help you reach your financial goals to enable you to retire on your terms and continue to live the lifestyle that you are accustomed to.

It is *simple*—but not *easy*. It requires education. It requires discipline. It requires maintenance.

If we espouse a secret; the secret is there is no *one* solution, or single strategy every person could or should implement to ensure financial success. There is no one size fits all approach. There is no easy method or benchmark that every investor can reference to determine failure or success.

The secret is; there is no secret. Crafting a plan and incorporating wealth management takes work, and we do this work every day.

Setting Expectations

A great deal of educating people on wealth management and planning starts with setting realistic and achievable expectations. We would all like to stumble upon a low-risk investment opportunity that provides high yield, but these are unicorns—at best very rare, at worst potentially illegal.

Wealth management is a long, slow process built on compounding interest, discipline and consistency. Are there opportunities out there with potential huge payoffs? Yes, but these opportunities always carry risk—risk of losing everything. With our clients, we set goals, define risk tolerance and determine expectations as soon as possible.

Investing tests your resolve and at times requires you to act against your natural instincts. Most importantly, you need to accept the fact that you will make mistakes. The world's best investors have made hundreds of mistakes. This is no different than many other professions.

Physicians are not able to cure every patient who walks into their office. Peyton Manning is a future Hall of Fame quarterback and he threw more than 250 interceptions in his NFL career. Michael Jordan missed dozens of game winning shots. A Major-League baseball player making an out in 70 percent of his plate appearances over a 15-year career will be recognized as an elite hitter.

Warren Buffett is widely regarded as one of the most successful investors of all time. Yet, as Buffett is willing to admit, even the best investors make mistakes. Buffett's legendary annual letters to his Berkshire Hathaway shareholders tell the tales of his biggest investing mistakes. Berkshire Hathaway underperformed the S&P 500 in 2015 with the flagship BRK.A shares down 11.47 percent compared with a 0.21 percent increase in the S&P 500 (we will tell you in Lesson Four why comparing to the S&P 500 is not generally the right call, anyway). The difference in total return versus its benchmark is even more pronounced–more than 13 percentage points–since Berkshire does not pay a dividend.

What do these professionals have in common? They never dwell on mistakes, rather they learn from failure. They developed an uncanny ability to maintain a forward-looking perspective.

The same is required of wealth management. Not every call will be a home run. You will lose along the way—but if you learn from your mistakes and mitigate your risks, you will win in the long run. Like a professional athlete, you should set goals and work towards achieving what is most important. You will lose a few games—even in a championship season.

Answering the Questions on Everyone's Minds

We all have questions about money. We all worry about money. Financial conflicts touch our lives every day. What we do for our clients is try to alleviate some of the stress caused by money. We talk to people every day. We answer questions from our clients, our friends, our family like:

Do I have enough money?

What does "enough" even mean?

Will I have enough to retire when I want to?

Do I know how much money I need to live the lifestyle I want in retirement?

Can I afford to fund my children's education?

Can I afford to help take care of my parents as they get older?

Can I give more time and money to a cause I am passionate about?

When will I be able to work when I want to (rather than needing to work a fixed/full schedule)?

Our objective is simple (not easy): this book provides guidance to help answer the questions people have been asking for years. This book answers questions people ask in their 20s, 30s, 40s, 50s, 60s, 70s and even 80s.

Our firm, our team, our advisors all work with individuals to meet their specific goals by focusing on education and understanding. You are far more likely to follow a plan you understand. You are far more likely to follow and trust a plan with clear goals.

We see a significant part of our role as being teachers. We answer questions and educate our clients on all aspects of their wealth management and planning. This book is a summary of what we know. It will serve as a primer for you to get started or to better educate yourself on your own current plan.

Where to Start

We believe everyone needs to engage in *Wealth Management* to ensure they adequately plan for their financial future.

What is *Wealth Management*?

Wealth Management is taking everything into account concerning your wealth. It includes investments; determining how to invest; when to invest; how much to invest; how much risk to take now—and how much risk to take later. Wealth management includes financial planning; saving and spending; taxes you must pay now—and taxes you may have to pay later. Wealth management includes protecting your assets; planning for the future with insurance and estate planning. Wealth management is having a plan in place so you have a course to stick to when you're unsure what to do during the next financial crisis (there will be another).

Having a plan is not enough—you must stay with your plan and adapt it as your life changes. We will discuss the most important components of your plan in detail, and how wealth management plays a key role in later Lessons of this book.

Our experiences have shown that the hardest part is getting started.

The following information includes Lessons we believe anyone—no matter where they happen to be in their life, and no matter how much or how little they know about investments—will find helpful.

This book is a resource guide. You can review the table of contents and see what Lessons are most interesting to you and jump right in, or you can start from the beginning.

We start with Part One: Investing 101, a valuable resource or refresher, that reviews the most common investing terms you will run into. In Lesson One we discuss basic terms, intermediate concepts and finally the more advanced items like alternatives, commodities, real estate, hedge funds and more.

In the next Lesson, we provide a history lesson on the U.S. markets—to illustrate how history has shaped and continues to shape the field. We provide summaries about market performance over the last century to provide a historic perspective on investing over a long term. We review concepts for investing in up, down and sideways markets. We take a deep dive into diversification and how to view long-term and short-term strategies.

In Part Two: How Do I Find the Right Advisor (or Do I Even Need an Advisor)?—we provide two Lessons detailing how it may be beneficial for you to work with the right trusted advisor, or team of advisors, to benefit you more in the long run than going alone. We show how professional advice can help mitigate the risks associated with personal cognitive biases that often trip individual investors—pros and amateurs alike. We discuss many of the most common pitfalls that affect investor returns and we review many common outdated procedures and/or concepts you can avoid to better position yourself for success. We provide a deep dive into the importance of seeking out objective investment advice from trusted sources. We start out by laying out the most common options for professional investment guidance. We review how to choose an advisor by educating you on how certain advisors differ from others.

Part Three: Wealth Management Strategy and Your Financial Plan, includes instructions on wealth management and investing strategies. You will find helpful information on how to manage your wealth strategically and how to adopt a winning mindset that can help you avoid the most common investing mistakes. The final Lesson provides detailed information on how to build and maintain your plan for investing success.

We review where to start, how to maintain, develop, and implement a wealth management plan that suits your needs. We include all the elements—and how having a good plan in place can alleviate fear, panic and stress. To go along with our discussion on transparency—we do not offer a perfect plan. There is no such thing as a perfect plan—and you will learn why.

We trust this book will be a helpful resource for you and we thank you in advance for taking time out of your busy schedule to read our work. We strongly believe everyone will get something out of this book. If nothing else, you will have armed yourself with information on where to start...or how to review your current plan to determine if you are on the right track.

Your next steps will be simple...but not easy. Good luck.

PART I

Investing 101

"Learning never exhausts the mind."
—Leonardo da Vinci

We strongly believe that thoughtful engagement in your wealth management starts with education—you must learn about basic investment terms and options.

If you think about retirement savings as a game—simply planning to budget and save money would be akin to checkers. If you actively engage in wealth management, you step up from checkers to chess.

In this Lesson, we will provide you a quick education by defining and explaining some of the basic pieces that make up investing and wealth management. Our goal is to lay out the most common concepts, provide a brief definition and describe why an investor would consider it—and potentially most important, why they would not.

For some of you, some of the terms may be new—for others, it will be helpful to review what you already know. In the long run, this can also be useful to you as a quick and easy to reference guide.

Learn Investment Terminology

"Know what you own, and know why you own it."
—Peter Lynch, American investor, philanthropist
and mutual fund manager of the Magellan Fund at Fidelity.

As Mr. Lynch states above—learning about *what* is in your investment portfolio is important. Equally important is learning the *why*. The following information is provided to help you with some of the basic, intermediate and more complex pieces that make up most investment portfolios. We describe what it is; how it is structured; and why you might consider utilizing the product, and finally why it may not work for everyone.

Stocks

 When we think of investing, usually the thing to come to mind first is a stock, which can also be called an "equity"—but how often do we revisit what a stock actually is? Remind yourself now:

What are they? A type of security providing investors with ownership in a corporation.

How are they structured? Publicly-traded stocks trade on an exchange, and each corporation has a limited number of shares available for purchase. Basic forces of supply and demand influence the perceived value of a company, particularly over short periods of time. Analysts will use sophisticated financial modeling tools to determine a fair long term valuation for a company, and ultimately the stock. A prevalent component of stock valuation is to determine the present value of future estimated cash flows. Clearly this requires making assumptions of growth rates, and can include a variety of tools beyond the scope of this chapter.

Why would an investor purchase? Stocks offer investors the greatest potential for growth over long periods of time.

Why would an investor avoid? Investing in stocks comes with a high level of risk. Investors are much more likely to lose all or a portion of their investment in a single company. The risk of investing in stocks can be reduced through diversification (owning many stocks, across different industries), however investors do need to be prepared to experience large swings in the value of their stock investments. Many individuals lack the risk tolerance to handle the emotional roller coaster of stock ownership.

Bonds

Generally, the safe haven for the risk-averse investor is the bond. You probably remember that bonds are safer than stocks, but you may not remember much else. Take a minute to review.

What are they? A debt security, commonly issued by a municipality or corporation, which will pay investors a fixed rate of interest for a defined period of time. The investor will have their principal returned by the lender, once the bond has matured.

How are they structured? Interest from the bond will be taxed as ordinary income if lent to a corporation. Municipalities may qualify to issue debt providing tax-free income to investors. The rate of interest an investor receives is dictated by taxability of income, credit worthiness of the issuer, period of time until maturity, and current economic conditions. A bond can be issued with a callable feature, allowing the issuer to return you principal prior to the stated maturity date. The issuer will be required to pay a premium for this feature.

Why would an investor purchase? Predictable income stream, in certain circumstances income is tax free. Lower risk profile compared to stocks. Provide stability to a larger investment portfolio.

Why would an investor avoid? Limited return. Credit risk if issuer defaults or simply goes out of business. Limited liquidity—unlike stocks, bonds typically have a sizeable spread between purchase and sale price. Interest rate risk current market value of bonds can decline in value if interest rates rise, which could negatively impact an investor wishing to sell prior to maturity.

Mutual Funds

The ubiquitous mutual fund used to be the single most popular diversification product in all investing. The concept of a mutual fund is easy, but the devil is in the details: like how is it allocated and what are the fees?

What are they? A company that pools money from a group of investors and invests in securities such as stocks, bonds, or a combination of the two.

How are they structured? There are two general types of mutual funds on the market. Open-end funds are what you know as a mutual fund. They don't have a limit as to how many shares they can issue. When an investor purchases shares in a mutual fund, more shares are created, and when somebody sells his or her shares, those shares are taken out of circulation.

Closed-end funds look similar but they are very different. A closed-end fund functions much more like an exchange traded fund than a mutual fund. They are launched through an IPO in order to raise money and then traded in the open market just like a stock or an ETF. They only issue a set number of shares and, although their value is also based on the NAV, the actual price of the fund is affected by supply and demand, allowing it to trade at prices above or below its real value.

Why would an investor purchase? Professional management, potential diversification (a fund typically owns 50-200 securities), liquidity, and comparative low cost of entry (an inexpensive way to own a basket of securities vs. purchasing each of the underlying securities individually).

Why would an investor avoid? Potential tax-inefficiency if the fund is owned in a non-retirement account, particularly for high net worth investors in the top two tax brackets. Mutual funds must distribute income and capital gains on to investors; therefore, it is possible to have a tax liability in a calendar year *when your fund loses money*. When compared to an exchange traded fund, the ongoing management fees associated with investing in many mutual funds can be high.

Stock Mutual Funds

What are they? A mutual fund which owns a pool of individual stocks.

How are they structured? Stock funds can own U.S. or foreign companies. The objective can be very broad, such as investing in growth companies, dividend paying stocks, or small company stocks. A stock fund can track an index, or have a very specific niche in which it operates. The fund can limit purchases to a specific sector, industry, region of the world or country.

Why would an investor purchase? Investors are typically hiring a manager with an expertise in the category where the fund invests. An investor may not have the time or desire to follow a portfolio of individual stocks; therefore, they take advantage of the professional management offered by a mutual fund. Stock funds can reduce risk by offering a low-cost method of diversification in a portfolio via ownership of a basket of securities.

Why would an investor avoid? Stock funds are professionally managed; therefore, you are paying for the service. Fees can act as a drag on investment performance, with open-end mutual funds typically charging higher expenses higher than index funds. A manager will attempt to outperform a benchmark by purchasing and selling securities. Trading will generate gains, which must be distributed to the shareholder for the fund to maintain a favorable tax status. Investors in the highest tax brackets owning mutual funds in a non-retirement account face the possibility of a substantial tax drag impacting net returns. Affluent individuals in this category should monitor the turnover and the tax cost associated with an actively managed stock fund.

Bond Mutual Funds

What are they? A mutual fund that owns a pool of individual bonds.

How is it structured? A bond fund could own short, intermediate or long-term bonds. The objective can include high income, total return, or principal preservation. Bond funds can invest in junk (low quality), investment grade corporates, foreign debt, government or municipal debt.

Why would an investor purchase? Investors use bond funds as a low-risk vehicle to minimize volatility and generate income. Liquidity is typically not a problem with bond funds; but this is not always the case with individual bonds. An appropriate bond fund could reduce portfolio risk via greater diversification in a cost-effective manner.

Why would an investor avoid? Unlike an individual bond, there is no defined maturity date with a bond fund. As a result, investors have less assurance that their full principal will be returned upon liquidation. Income streams can be less predictable. While bond funds do offer professional management, there is a cost associated with hiring a fund manager.

Stocks, bonds and mutual funds are the most basic pieces. Most everyone has at least a passing understanding of how they work— but perhaps less understanding of how they work together. The following pieces are more complex. Exchange traded funds (ETFs) are important components and we take a relatively deep dive below explaining their function.

Exchange Traded Funds (ETFs)

What are they? An ETF, or exchange traded fund, is a marketable security that tracks an index, a commodity, bonds, or a basket of assets like an index fund.

How is it structured? Unlike mutual funds, an ETF trades like a common stock on a stock exchange. ETFs experience price changes throughout the day as they are bought and sold.

Why would an investor purchase? ETFs typically have higher daily liquidity and lower fees than mutual fund shares, making them an attractive alternative for individual investors. ETFs give the investor the opportunity to buy or sell an entire portfolio of stocks or other securities in a single security, just like buying or selling a share of a single stock.

Pros and Cons of ETFs

- **Passive diversification:** By buying a single unit of an ETF, investors can get exposure to all the securities that make up the underlying index. ETFs also reflect the performance of different sectors in the market, which can help enhance the diversification benefits of investor portfolios. However, keep in mind that diversification does not eliminate the risk of investment losses.

- **Transparency of price:** Since ETFs trade like stocks, their prices change and new prices are available to investors at all times during trading hours.

- **Tax efficiency:** When mutual funds realize a capital gain, they are obligated to distribute those gains to investors on an annual basis, which is a taxable event for non-retirement accounts. ETFs usually realize capital gains when changes are made to the benchmarks (index funds) they track. Index portfolios generally have lower turnover than actively managed funds, which makes ETFs ideal for taxable accounts. ETFs may also realize capital gains if the share price of the ETF rises. Consult a tax professional to better understand the tax implications of ETFs.

- **Potential cost advantages:** Unlike many actively managed mutual funds, there are no front-end or deferred sales charges with ETFs, which are bought and sold like stocks. On the exchange, the investor pays brokerage costs and the spread between the buying and selling price, which may be lower cost than the front-end load and transaction fees of mutual funds.

- **Protection against cash drag:** Cash drag is the return lost when an open-end fund manager must keep cash on hand or sell assets to redeem shares. ETFs don't need to hold cash in anticipation of redemptions, which may minimize the cash drag effect. Long-term investors may be affected most by cash drag.

- **Brokerage costs:** ETFs are bought and sold through a broker which typically results in brokerage costs every time a buy or sell transaction occurs. Brokerage costs incurred may be a significant percentage of the investment for smaller transactions.

- **Variable Liquidity:** Liquidity for ETFs varies widely, depending on not just the trading volume of the fund but also the liquidity of the underlying securities it holds. Typically, the more exotic the asset class and financial instruments used, the less liquid the ETF and the higher the spread.

- **Relative newness:** Some ETFs, especially those that offer exposure to more exotic asset classes (which are riskier), are relatively new and have been around for only a few years, which may pose a few drawbacks in terms of historical data availability.

- **Limited selection:** The limited availability of ETFs in certain categories can be a disadvantage for investors. Holding an exchange-traded fund does not ensure a profitable outcome and all investing involves risk, including the loss of the entire principal. Since each ETF is different, investors should read the prospectus and consider this information carefully before investing. The prospectus can be obtained from your financial professional or the ETF provider and contains complete information, including investment objectives, risks, charges and expenses. ETF risks include, but are not limited to, market risk, market trading risk, liquidity risk, imperfect benchmark correlation, leverage, and any other risk associated with the underlying securities. There is no guarantee that any fund will achieve its investment objective. In addition to ETF expenses, brokerage costs apply. Fees are charged regardless of profitability and may result in depletion of assets. The market price of ETFs traded on the secondary market is subject to the forces of supply and demand and thus independent of the NAV. This can result in the market price trading at a premium or discount to the NAV which will affect an investor's value. The market prices of ETFs can fluctuate as a result of several factors, such as security-specific factors or general investor sentiment. Therefore, investors should be aware of the prospect of market fluctuations and the impact it may have on the market price. ETF trading may be halted due to market conditions, impacting an investor's ability to sell the ETF.

More About Fees, Expense Ratios of ETFs, Index Funds, and Active Funds

ETFs normally have lower expense ratios when compared with traditional mutual funds. This happens because managers of actively-managed funds tend to charge more for their expertise in picking investments.

We will look at large-cap funds, as this is the broadest category for us to compare. Large-cap funds are funds that invest primarily in large-cap U.S. stocks. Stocks in the top 70 percent of the capitalization of the U.S. equity market are defined as large-cap. An index mutual fund is a fund that tracks a particular index and attempts to match its returns. An active fund is a fund whose manager analyzes the market and selects investments in order to maximize return. Expense ratio data is from Morningstar's open-end database. ETF and index fund expense ratios are from the domestic large-cap ETF and domestic large-cap index fund categories, respectively. All expense ratios are prospectus net expense ratios. The prospectus net expense ratio is the percentage of fund assets paid for administrative, management, 12b-1 advertising fees and other expenses. The expense ratio does not reflect the fund's brokerage costs.

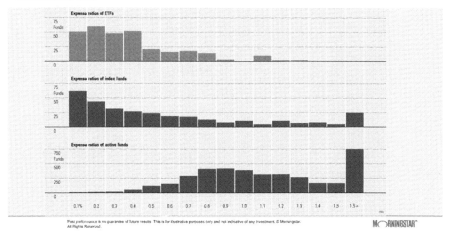

Expense Ratios of Large-Caps: ETFs, Index Funds, and Active Funds
As of December 2016

See appendix for magnified chart

The image illustrates the distribution of expense ratios for large-cap ETFs, index mutual funds and actively-managed mutual funds. For actively-managed funds, it appears that expense ratios are higher on average, with many funds exceeding 1.5 percent. Expense ratios for large-cap index funds, however, vary widely from 0.1 percent to over 1.5 percent. The average active fund investing in large-cap stocks carries an expense ratio of 1.24 percent of the investor's holdings, and the average index fund, 0.72 percent.

Expense ratios for large-cap ETFs appear to be lower on average, and are typically concentrated between 0.1 percent and 1.0 percent. The average expense ratio for large-cap ETFs is 0.42 percent. The difference in costs between ETFs and traditional funds may not seem substantial, but these costs add up over time. It is important that investors evaluate their investment goals when selecting a fund.

Separately Managed Accounts

 What are they? An investment strategy presented to the affluent as an alternative to mutual funds. Rather than owning a single pooled investment, the investor will actually own a large number of individual stocks.

How are they structured? A separately managed account will typically have a defined strategy, investing in a specific asset class and/or style (Large Cap growth, International stocks, Municipal Bonds, etc.). The custodian holding your assets will create a new account and provide power of attorney to the asset manager making trades on a client's behalf. A client's advisor is not making investment decisions. Trading is delegated to a large institution with a perceived expertise investing in a particular asset class or industry. Minimums range from $100,000 to $250,000 and could be higher in some cases.

Why would an investor purchase? One appeal is professional management from a firm with an expertise in a very specific style of investing. When comparing a separately managed account to a mutual fund, the former does offer the opportunity for greater tax efficiency. An investor could be purchasing someone else's tax liability if the mutual fund purchased has embedded gains. For example, if ABC growth fund has owned XYZ stock for 20 years, XYZ stock is going to have substantial gains which will be passed on to the investor that purchased the fund a few weeks ago. The separately managed account investors will have a cost basis attributable to their actual purchase date of the underlying securities.

Why would an investor avoid? Separately managed accounts are typically more expensive than mutual funds and exchange traded funds. Fees range from 1.35 percent to 2.25 percent of assets in the program. A client will commonly own 75-100 positions with very small balances in a defined strategy. While separately managed accounts may offer year-end tax harvesting, if the strategy has high turnover it may not be tax efficient. While managed accounts are often presented as a strategy for the affluent, keep in mind they are built to serve the masses, lacking customization or a willingness to work with an existing portfolio.

As we continue to review different aspects of wealth management—we continue to get more complex. If stocks, bonds and mutual funds are basic, and ETFs and SMAs are intermediate, then the following pieces would be advanced. "Alternatives" like Real Estate, Hedge Funds, Private Equity, etc.—these components do not fit into all plans because:

- They achieve different goals than the pieces above

- They can be expensive with complicated fee structures

- They may be illiquid—tough to convert to cash

- They could incur much higher risk of losing a majority, or all, of the principal invested

Even though they may be complex, it is important to understand how these function, especially if you will consider them as part of your wealth management strategy.

Before we describe specific alternatives—let's briefly review the term "alternatives" in general.

Alternative Investments

What are they? "Alternative investment" is a broad term encompassing a wide range of investment strategies that fall outside traditional asset classes. They generally include non-traded investment programs, commodities (like gold and other precious metals), currency, hedge funds, long/short, and other market-neutral strategies.

How are they structured? They can be liquid in a mutual fund; or non-traded structures, private equity, hedge funds, real estate investment trusts, commodities, as well as real assets such as precious metals, rare coins, wine and art.

Why would an investor purchase? Alternatives usually represent investments that have a low correlation to the S&P 500. The lack of correlation between the two helps dampen portfolio volatility. Because of this lack of correlation, many large institutional funds like pensions and private endowments, allocate a healthy portion (typically in the 10-20 percent range) of their portfolios to alternatives. Inclusion of non-correlated assets should decrease volatility and increase overall diversification. These tools are further used to customize investment portfolios to meet the objectives of the individual.

Why would an investor avoid? It may be difficult with some alternative investments to determine the current market value of the investment. They may also be relatively illiquid. In some instances, these investments may have limited historical risk and return data, and the cost of purchase and sale may be high.

We could literally write a book on alternative investments alone—but to keep this Lesson manageable, we cover the most common alternatives: commodities, real estate, hedge funds, private equity, structured products and annuities.

Commodities

You would have to have been living under a rock for the last 10-20 years to have not seen or heard at least one commercial or radio advertisement advocating a commodity. Often that commodity is gold. Gold has such staunch advocates that it has spawned the term "Gold Bug"—for someone who attempts to hedge their portfolio against weakness in the U.S. Dollar, inflation and deflation by relying on gold. On the other side, gold has detractors who speak and write almost exclusively on dispelling myths and discussing why the Gold Bugs are wrong.

The truth is—there can be a justification for utilizing gold (or other commodities) in your portfolio. However, you should understand the how and the why.

What are they? Metals (Gold, Silver, Copper), grains and other food, or financial instruments such as foreign currencies.

How are they structured? Typically, commodities are owned *via* futures contracts, which is an agreement to buy a certain quantity of a commodity at a point in the future. Futures contracts are typically traded on the floor of an exchange. Today, commodities can be purchased via an ETF or mutual fund specializing in a specific commodity or basket of commodities.

Why would an investor purchase? Commodities are often viewed as a hedge against inflation, and they are purchased by certain investors who may be concerned about the strength of the U.S. dollar. Correlation to traditional stocks and bonds is typically low, therefore an allocation to commodities has the potential to lower overall portfolio volatility.

Why would an investor avoid? While a small allocation to commodities may reduce volatility in a portfolio, commodities themselves tend to be one of the most volatile asset classes an investor could access. The SEC does not regulate commodity futures, therefore investing in the asset class is typically not suitable for the average investor. An investment in commodities can generate a K1, therefore taxation can be very complex.

Real Estate

 For many people, the majority of their net worth is tied up in their home and business property—more than in any other investment. Compared to stocks, bonds and most other investment vehicles, real estate is a highly tangible asset—and an emotional one. We raise our children there; our vacations often revolve around it and it's our piece of a beach or mountain—a place we love. Nothing in a financial portfolio provides quite the same warm feelings, memories and experiences wrapped up in real estate.

There can also be a financial benefit to owning real estate such as tax, income and diversification. It is important to understand the role that real estate plays in your overall wealth management plan. Like any other asset, it comes with advantages and disadvantages. It can be an important part of your overall portfolio and wealth management plan.

Using real estate, fortunes can be won... and lost during market downturns. Often this is because of leverage—as most real estate is bought with mortgages, the leverage factor can work to build fortunes quickly, but also to decimate them quickly as well. In our practice, we have seen more clients get in financial trouble with leveraged real estate than any other investment.

Real estate is often touted as a hedge against the securities market—but 2008 demonstrated this is not always the case—as the real estate market crashed along with the securities markets... and, in many places around the U.S., took longer to rebound. Because of this, along with illiquidity and mortgage interest payments coming due, we saw many otherwise financially secure families suffer greatly.

What is it? Real estate is property comprised of land and the buildings on it as well as the natural resources of the land.

How is it structured? Real estate can be grouped into three broad categories based on its use: residential, commercial and industrial. Examples of residential real estate include undeveloped land, houses, condominiums and townhomes; examples of commercial real estate are office buildings, warehouses and retail store buildings; and examples of industrial real estate are factories, mines and farms.

Why would an investor purchase? The price of real estate historically has increased in value over longer periods; say at least 10-year time periods. Therefore, purchasing real estate can be one of the great long-term investments a person can make. Benefits include the ability to use leverage to take advantage of low interest rate environments, the ability to create predictable income streams with rental properties, the ability to take advantage of tax benefits like depreciation, and the potential increase the value of the real estate itself.

Why would an investor avoid? Depending on the expense and value of real estate holdings, a portfolio can become over-weighted by real estate, creating possible exposure to a sharp decline in the real estate market. You may also have the issue of a lack of liquidity and cash flow in retirement based on the size and type of the real estate in your portfolio.

The real estate pendulum swings back and forth between being in vogue and passé. Usually it depends on where the securities markets are. Real estate can be a useful and valuable asset—it can also be a major headache. Rather that owning actual real estate, many investors utilize Real Estate Investment Trusts (REITs).

Real Estate Investment Trusts (REITS)

What are they? A trust that owns a pool of income producing real estate assets. REITs may invest in office buildings, shopping centers, storage facilities, apartments, hotels, mortgages, or loans.

How are they structured? A REIT buys properties and operates the properties as part of a larger investment portfolio. Typically, REITs will distribute income to investors, and trade on an exchange. REITs can also be purchased in a non-traded format. If this is the case investors should expect to receive a premium for tying up their funds.

Why would an investor purchase? Investors have the opportunity to diversify the risk of owning real estate, by holding multiple properties in various regions in the U.S. and potentially internationally. Income streams can be attractive, while capital appreciation may be a secondary objective. A pooled real estate investment does not require the investor to accept the responsibilities of management and maintenance that may be required with a direct investment in real estate. REITs may also offer an added layer of diversification in a larger investment portfolio.

Why would an investor avoid? If an investor purchases a non -traded REIT, they are unlikely to have liquidity, meaning the investment cannot be sold. If economic conditions deteriorate, a lack of liquidity can be detrimental. Transaction costs, financing, and operating costs can be substantial with real estate investment trusts. Non-traded REITs purchased through a broker can charge as much as 10 percent of the investment up front. Tax rules can be complex, as distributions could be treated as ordinary income, a return of capital, or a combination of the two.

Hedge Funds

 The term "hedge funds" is ubiquitous, but many people do not understand what a hedge fund actually is. Let's look past famous hedge fund managers, and acquaintances dropping the term in dinner conversations, and learn the details about how they work and why they may be useful.

What are they? The concept has some similarities to a mutual fund. Hedge funds pool money from individual investors to purchase assets. Strategies can vary drastically; some may have the objective of reduced volatility with a return stream which is not correlated to traditional financial markets. Many hedge funds strive to achieve maximum return, investing in niche markets, or using leverage to enhance upside. Hedge funds have high minimum investment requirements, are not liquid, and face fewer regulatory requirements.

How are they structured? As previously mentioned, the structure of hedge funds varies widely. Many hedge funds hold investments that are illiquid and difficult to value. Valuation of the fund typically comes from an independent source, and is provided on a quarterly basis, as opposed to a publicly traded security offering daily valuation. Given the lack of liquidity and risks associated with hedge funds, they typically require investors to meet minimum income and net worth requirements.

Why would an investor purchase? A broad answer is difficult due to the wide range of potential objectives for the funds. The answer generally falls into one of three categories: 1) Greater upside (albeit with greater risk); 2) Access to niche investments not available through traditional methods; 3) Opportunity to achieve returns which may not correlate with traditional stocks or bonds. An appeal does exist to gain access to certain managers with a lengthy track record of success. These individuals may no longer run traditional mutual funds, therefore the only way to access their expertise is *via* the hedge fund channel.

Why would an investor might avoid? Lack of liquidity or transparency, limited regulation and risk are several reasons why hedge funds are not appropriate for most investors. While each of the previously mentioned characteristics are reasons why many high net worth investors avoid hedge funds, none are the number one reason many pass on the opportunity. Hedge funds are famous for their high fee structure. Management fees range from 1-2 percent of assets, in addition to a performance fee of 20 percent of the fund's profit. *Example: (this is for illustrative purposes, we acknowledge the math is not quite this simple) a $10,000 investment obtains a gross return of 20 percent and is now worth $12,000. A 2 percent fee is $240, 20 percent incentive on $2,000 gain is $400. $640 in fees paid on $12,000 is 5.34 percent.*

Since the start of 2005 through 2015, the HFRX Global Hedge Fund Index and HFRX Equity Hedge Index (two investable indices widely used as benchmarks in the hedge fund industry) have posted negative returns (-1 percent and -6.4 percent respectively). Over that same time period, the Barclays Aggregate Bond Index was up 62.1 percent and the S&P 500 up 97.6 percent. The argument for hedge funds is not typically just about returns, but lower volatility, low correlation and absolute return when equities go down. The difficulty is that the managers who achieve those goals are few and far between.

Private Equity

What is it? Private equity funds are typically structured as pools of capital that invest primarily in private companies. The intention of the strategy is to create value in these private enterprises by cutting costs, improving logistics/synergies, and selling non-performing assets (making the company more 'lean' in the attempt to generate additional cash flow). Through a private equity fund, a number of investors combine their capital, enabling the managers of the fund to actively make investments in various companies on the investor's behalf. This asset class can contain both equity and debt securities in operating companies that typically are not publicly traded. Most private equity deals come in the form of a *"private equity fund"* as most institutions/individuals lack the necessary resources to identify and monitor privately held businesses.

How is it structured? Many private equity funds are structured as limited partnerships (LPs) or limited liability companies (LLCs) which are in turn are managed by an LP general partner or LLC manager. This general partner/manager will identify and perform extensive due diligence on potential companies, all with the discretion to make investments for the fund. Private equity funds usually have a main investment theme or strategy that focuses on businesses in certain industries, geographic location, and varying valuations/size. Most private equity investments are illiquid and can be difficult to value (mainly because the underlying companies being purchased are not public and therefore do not have readily available financials). The fee structure is very like that of a hedge fund, meaning 2 percent ongoing annual management fee as well as a 20 percent fee for gross profits upon the sale of the company.

Why would an investor purchase? An investor would typically purchase a stake in PE firm/strategy for many of the same reasons when considering a hedge fund:

- Greater upside returns (albeit with greater risk due to illiquidity/leverage)

- Access to niche investments (private businesses) not available through traditional methods

- Opportunity to achieve returns which may not correlate with traditional stocks/bonds

Why would an investor avoid? Much like any investment, there are many potential risks to investing in private equity. Some of those risks include considerable capital commitments, lack of liquidity, lack of transparency, high ongoing management/incentive fees, use of leverage, potential conflicts of interest, minimal control over investments, dependence on key management, lack of regulation (albeit improving), tax considerations, and wide-ranging performance amongst all PE funds.

Our take is that the illiquidity profile of these deals is the most burdensome hurdle to overcome (especially in a world where you can invest in most areas of the globe through a daily liquid/traded fund). A typical PE fund can take anywhere from 4-8 years before its eventual 'exit' (liquidity event). A client investing in a PE fund needs to understand that his/her money can be locked up for a period of eight years while receiving little to no income distributions (PE structure lacks income/yield component).

Another challenge for investors to overcome is lack of full transparency. This has slightly improved since the financial crisis of 2008-2009 with the passing of the "Dodd Frank" regulations. Title IV of "Dodd-Frank" requires all PE firms with more than $150 million in assets to register with the SEC (this began in 2012).

Lastly, investors may look to avoid PE funds largely due to the performance divergence between the top and bottom quartile managers. According to Preqin, a firm that indexes PE returns, an individual with a top quartile PE fund manager would have earned more than 2.6x that of an investor with a second quartile manager, and lost money investing with a bottom (fourth) quartile manager. An investor with $10,000 invested in PE funds, would have accumulated an extra $56,180 (per every $10,000 invested) by investing in the top vs. second quartile managers (From Sept 2000-2014).

Structured Products

What are they? Structured products, as described by the Financial Industry Regulatory Authority (FINRA), are securities derived from or based on a single security, a basket of securities, an index, a commodity, a debt issuance and/or a foreign currency. They are a hybrid between two asset classes typically issued in the form of a corporate bond or a certificate of deposit but, instead of having a pre-determined rate of interest, the return is linked to the performance of an underlying asset class.

How is it structured? As this definition suggests, there are multiple types of structured products. These variations include certain products offering full protection of the principal invested while others may offer limited or no protection of principal. Most structured products offer the potential to pay an interest or coupon rate above the prevailing market rate and are used as tools by high net worth investors for portfolio diversification. Structured product sales began in the 1980s. These investment vehicles arose from the needs of companies seeking options for debt issuance. Here, companies can transfer risk, for a fee. Structured products provide investors with highly targeted investments that are tied to a specific risk profile, return requirements and market expectations.

How Structured Products Work Similar to a zero-coupon bond, often, no interest payments are made during the life of the security. In most cases, the investor bypasses traditional payments in exchange for participation in the underlying asset class of that particular issue. Any payments earned by the investor, such as through market performance or the return of principal, are determined by the specific terms of each individual deal and are made on the set maturity date. Moreover, many structured products are designed by combining two components, a zero-coupon bond, providing for the principal return, and a call option on the underlying asset, allowing investors to participate in the potential appreciation of the referenced asset.

Why would an investor purchase? Structured products are designed to provide increased control over risk and returns through leverage, principal protection, enhanced returns, risk management and customized access to asset classes or investment types. Their payments are typically linked to the performance of underlying market indices or securities, rather than fixed coupons, and they are customizable for specific investment objectives. Investors in structured products are typically seeking to maximize returns on an investment strategy, manage risk exposure to capital classes, hedge market risk, or customize solutions for complex investment objec-

Types of Structured Strategies

- **Enhanced Yield Notes**—Designed to provide enhanced yield relative to comparable fixed income securities with the same credit rating and maturity. In this category, digital notes, auto-callable notes and callable yield notes are some of the offerings.
- **Growth-Oriented Notes**—Designed to provide levered upside participation in the gains of the underlying asset; the maximum return may be capped or uncapped. In this category, accelerated return notes and market plus notes are some of the offerings.
- **Market-Linked Securities**—Designed to provide investors a return of their full initial investment if held to maturity. In this category, market-linked notes and market-linked certificates of deposit are some of the offerings.
- **Access Notes**—Designed to provide investors exposure to an underlying asset class or index that may be difficult to access through traditional investment vehicles.

tives. While structured products may potentially outperform typical fixed interest rate bonds, it is important to remember that they are subject to risks, including, among others, the credit risk of their issuer and potential underperformance in certain circumstances.

Why would an investor avoid?

- **Credit Risk:** Structured products are unsecured debt obligations of the issuer. As a result, they are subject to the risk of default by the issuer. The creditworthiness of the issuer will affect its ability to pay interest and repay principal. The financial condition and credit rating of the issuer are, therefore, important considerations. The credit rating, if any, pertains to the issuer and is not indicative of the market risk of the structured product or underlying asset. If a structured issue provides principal protection or a minimum return, any such guarantee rests on the credit quality of the issuer. Those issued by banks in the forms of CDs may also provide FDIC insurance with standard coverage limitations.

- **Liquidity Risk:** Structured products are generally not listed on an exchange or may be thinly traded. As a result, there may be a limited secondary market for these products, making it difficult for investors to sell them prior to maturity. Investors who need to sell structured products prior to maturity are likely to receive less than the amount they invested. Therefore, structured products with longer maturities are subject to greater liquidity risk. The price that someone is willing to pay for structured products in a secondary sale will be influenced by market forces and other factors that are hard to predict. Sometimes, a broker-dealer affiliate of the issuer may make a market for the resale of structured products prior to maturity; but the price it is willing to pay will be adversely affected by the commissions paid by the issuer on the initial sale of the structured products and the issuer's hedging costs. Some structured products have lock-up periods prohibiting their sale during such periods. Persons who invest in structured products should have the financial means to hold them until maturity.

- **Pricing Risk:** Structured products are difficult to price since their value is tied to an underlying asset or basket of assets and there typically is no established trading market for structured products from which to determine a price.

- **Income Risk:** Structured products may not pay interest (or may not pay interest in regular amounts or at regular intervals), so they are not appropriate for investors looking for current income. Because the return paid on structured products at maturity is tied to the performance of a basket of assets and will be variable, it is possible that the return may be zero or significantly less than what investors could have earned on an ordinary, interest-bearing debt security. The return on structured products, if any, is subject to market and other risks related to the underlying assets.

- **Complexity and Derivatives Risk:** Structured products typically use leverage, options, futures, swaps and other derivatives, which involve special risks and additional complexity.

- **Pay-Out Structure Risk:** Some structured products impose limits, caps and barriers that affect their return potential. With barriers, a structured product may not offer any return if a barrier is broken or breached during the term of the structured product. Conversely, some structured products may not offer any return unless certain thresholds are achieved. Some structured products impose maximum return limits so even if the underlying assets generate a return greater than the stated limit or cap investors do not realize that excess return. Structured products also have participation rates that describe an investor's share in the return of the underlying assets. Participation rates below 100 percent mean that the investor will realize a return that is less than the return on the underlying assets.

Options

What are they? A contract giving the owner the right to buy or sell an asset at a specific price, at or prior to a specific future date. An option is a derivative, meaning the value is determined by an underlying asset. Examples of these assets are stocks, bonds, exchange traded funds, commodities, currencies, or stock indices.

How are they structured? Options have a variety of designs; explaining every type is beyond the scope of this Lesson. In the interest of simplicity, the focus will be limited to the most common form of options, the stock option. The security trades on an exchange, and each option trade represents a zero-sum game between the buyer and seller. A single contract represents 100 shares of a stock. Understanding the terminology within an option quote via an actual example may be an easier way to learn.

An investor deciding to buy an XYZ January 50 Call $1.85 suggests the following:

- XYZ is the name of the underlying stock

- January is the month which the option expires

- $50 represents the strike price for the option, the price at which the buyer of the option contract may buy the underlying stock

- Call identifies the type of option contract. In the example above the buyer of the call maintains the right to purchase 100 shares of XYZ stock at $50. If the stock runs to $60 or even $100, the investor would maintain the right to buy the stock at $50. The inverse strategy is to buy a put option, which is the right to sell a stock at a pre-determined strike price. An investor purchasing a put would anticipate the underlying stock declining in value.

- $1.85 is the price you pay per share for one contract, also commonly referred to as the option premium. A single option contract typically represents 100 shares, consequently the investor would pay $185 for this particular option.

Why would an investor purchase? Tremendous upside and leverage are the most common reasons.

Why would an investor avoid? Two big reasons:

1. **Risk**—Investors must understand the potential loss associated with options trading. Selling *put* options (selling a *put* option means you are granting the opposite party the right to sell a stock at a defined price. The seller of the put option has an obligation to buy the stock from the contra party. A stock price is not capped, consequently an investor's potential loss is unlimited) is arguably the most aggressive investment strategy one could pursue, considering the potential loss is *unlimited*. Purchasing a *call*, is an

option trade occurring with greater frequency. A *call* option expires worthless if the stock does not exceed the strike price. If the option does expire, the investor loses his or her entire investment.

2. **Finite Time-Period Equates to Speculation**—Investors recognize stocks tend to increase in value over time. Unfortunately, the appreciation is not linear, in many cases equites flatline for months or years (for example: investors referred to the period from 2000-2009 as the lost decade. The S&P 500 experienced two major corrections, equity investors with unfortunate timing experienced negligible returns during this timeframe). Equity returns tend to be concentrated over short periods of time. Unlike stocks, options are finite investments with a specific expiration date. An options trader is speculating they will be able to identify the proper time frame when a stock or stock index appreciates. The trader is attempting to successfully execute marketing timing. He or she must identify the correct time to purchase the option and recognize the appropriate time to close the trade.

Annuities

What are they? A contract between you and an insurance company, backed by the full faith and creditworthiness of that insurer. The insurance company will agree to make payments to you at some point in the future via a lump sum or as a series of payments over an agreed upon period time.

How are they structured? Annuities are typically structured to credit your account in one of three ways: 1) A fixed annuity designed to credit a minimum amount of interest annually 2) Variable annuity providing the investor with an option to invest in mutual funds. The payout is directly related to the success of the selected investments. 3) An Indexed annuity offered a form of crediting tied to an index such as the S&P 500.

Why would an investor purchase? In the accumulation phase: Tax deferred growth, no annual contribution limit. Some states provide unlimited asset protection as part of their state exemption statutes. Distribution phase: Offers the ability to create an income stream for life or a defined period. Reliable income stream designed to complement a pension, social security, or an investment portfolio.

Why would an investor avoid? Cost. An investor could be subject to an up-front commission of 5-10 percent of the initial investment. Annuities often have a surrender charge, meaning you must pay a fee to exit the policy if you attempt to do so within the first several years of the contract. Surrender periods commonly run from 7-10 years, with the surrender charge typically declining by 1 percent for every year you are in the contract. Annual fees are typically higher in annuity compared to a traditional investment account. Insurance charges, fund management fees, and insurance riders can increase the annual fee to 3-4 percent of assets.

Conclusion

The preceding information is provided to give you a quick summary of components and tools utilized in wealth management. How the tools are used depends on your goals, your appetite for risk and your timeline. Further, how you employ these tools will likely change depending on whether you are just starting out with your planning—or are getting close to retirement.

Knowing what the tools are is one thing—understanding how they work is another. To help illustrate, we use the next Lesson to provide a history of the markets. Having a passing knowledge of how the markets have worked historically will help you understand how investing fits into your overall wealth management.

The following Lesson illustrates some of the most prevalent trends of the last 100 years—but it is important to keep in mind, as all disclaimers and disclosures note: past performance does not promise specific future results.

You will see that, historically, the markets have been unpredictable yet have trended upwards. We will show you how allocating the tools in the previous Lessons can help mitigate the consequences of market unpredictability and work to build your wealth.

Keep Market History in Perspective

"It's been my experience...that the past always has a way of returning. Those who don't learn, or can't remember it, are doomed to repeat it."

–Steve Berry, best-selling author, history professor and Founder of History Matters Foundation

You have heard—those who refuse to learn history, are doomed to repeat it. This statement is relevant in many areas. Investing and wealth management are not excluded. It is important to know at least a passing history concerning the securities markets because knowing the history will help you avoid some of the past mistakes investors have made—sometimes over and over. A passing knowledge also demonstrates why the tortoise approach of slow and steady saving and investing works—while the rabbit approach of market timing and seeking home run investments is a recipe for disaster.

It is extremely important to understand—markets go up, but they also go down. You may understand that in theory, but in reality, when markets go down, some investors lose their focus.

"Should I go to cash?"

"Should I get out now and come back when things start to turn?"

"Should I sell low now and buy back in high?"

Nobody ever really asks that last question, but that may be the effect on their wealth if they follow the instincts indicated by the first two. See Lessons Four and Six for the data on how prevalent this is.

If you take nothing away from this Lesson but one point—remember that markets do go down. If you cannot live with the fact that there will be market declines—there will be recessions—then you should not be in the market. You are not ready.

Only when you can accept that historically market declines have been relatively short and have historically rebounded and you can remain disciplined—then you are ready.

If you know some of the history—you might consider skipping this Lesson and returning sometime later. But whether you read it now or later—do read it. Even if it serves as refresher on information you probably already know—the Lessons are important.

It is easy to say investing is all "buy low and sell high"—but executing that strategy is much more difficult when it is your wealth on the line. No matter what field you are in, you know that building and maintaining wealth is a challenge. No matter what your stage in life, when seeking to meet your financial goals, it is critical that your assets shoulder some of the burden. Unfortunately, we generally find that most investors do not have their investments working hard enough for them.

As the data below demonstrates, you don't have to hit a home run every time, but you need to get on base and avoid making outs to get a reasonable return over the long haul.

Understanding the history and terminology of the markets will help you navigate the playing field and avoid repeating past mistakes. It is *smart* to learn from your own mistakes—but it is *wise* to learn from the mistakes of others—and not to mention, much less painful.

Bull Markets, Bear Markets, Corrections

  Bull markets (up markets): many technically define a bull market as period of increase in value in the market of at least 20 percent. But there is more to it than that. Bull markets are characterized by optimism, investor confidence and expectations that strong results will continue. It's difficult to predict consistently when the trends in the market will change. Part of the difficulty is that psychological effects and speculation may sometimes play a large role in the markets.

Bear Markets (down markets) represent a market condition in which the prices of securities are falling, and widespread pessimism causes the negative sentiment to be self-sustaining. As investors anticipate losses in a bear market and selling continues, pessimism only grows. Although figures can vary, for many, **a downturn of 20 percent or more** in multiple broad market indexes, such as the Dow Jones Industrial Average (DJIA) or Standard & Poor's 500 Index (S&P 500), over at least a two-month period, is considered an entry into a bear market.

Market Corrections—A reverse movement, usually negative, of **at least 10 percent** in a stock, bond, commodity or index to adjust for an overvaluation. Corrections are generally temporary price declines interrupting an uptrend in the market or an asset. A correction has a shorter duration than a bear market or a recession, but it can be a precursor to either.

Those textbook definitions help us understand the technical side of market movements, but do little to address the psychological effects on investors. How emotion plays a major part in your investment decisions.

When talking with clients about market volatility, we often discuss emotion. Money, and specifically your money, is very personal and emotional to you. During bull markets and investor enthusiasm, emotion can often cause irrational decisions such as buying more of a particular security—not because the fundamentals suggest there is value, but simply because you have possibly felt short-term exuberance from gains and more of that feeling would seem logical. The problem is emotion can often negatively affect your portfolio strategy. While it is present in bull markets, we most often see the biggest problems arising during bear markets. Down markets force people to assess the damage in their portfolios more often, which leads to pain from seeing losses, which leads to even more monitoring of performance. It becomes a vicious cycle.

The natural instincts of investors are often wrong. Buy low and sell high often requires you to do the opposite of your instincts.

In today's world, we are all besieged with news and information at our fingertips. Investment advice and thoughts are now being blasted out to the masses in 140 characters or less. When markets are stable and calm or rising during a bull market period we see less *breaking news* and *instant* analysis. It is precisely at the time clients need guidance—corrections and/or bear markets that we have news headlines: "plunging equities," "Another crash is on the way," "death spiral for the markets" and on and on.

Investors who we have said are already emotionally tied to their hard-earned money (as they should be) are now being preyed upon from multiple media. This makes it very difficult to make sound financial decisions.

When clients contact us asking if they should change their strategy, we respond with one simple question. Has anything changed in your life since our last meeting that would alter your goals or change your tolerance for risk?

If the answer is *yes*, we will sit down and discuss how their investment portfolio is currently constructed—what type of return is expected as well as the type of volatility. If that no longer is inline, we will make the necessary changes. More often than not, the answer is *no*. "I'd still like to retire on X with X amount of money to last X amount of years and I am comfortable with losses of X." If that matches their current portfolio we will discuss the emotion of the markets and how best to take advantage of the environment.

Background on U.S. Markets

Most investors have reviewed or have even taken part in scientific studies. The sample size is one of the most important factors in determining the validity of any study. The same holds true for investing. Scientists are trained to review data dispassionately, but as we will discuss in future Lessons, most investors struggle with common behavioral psychology. These struggles cause them to base important investment decisions on information from short samples— leading to emotional and irrational decisions.

Basing investment strategies on one-year, three-year or even five-year sample sizes can lead to long-term headaches.

Below, we will look at over 90 years of historic data from the Dow Jones Industrial Average (DOW), and over 80 years' worth of data from the Standard and Poor 500 Index (S&P). We will also go outside the boundaries of the U.S. stock market and review 40 years of data from the Japanese Nikkei 225.

The DOW and the S&P 500

Any extended view of the DOW or the S&P shows that, over the long term, the securities markets have varied greatly year to year. That being said, both markets have historically trended upwards.

There are *up* periods and some *down* periods, and there are periods where the market has grinded along *sideways* while slowly inching higher. A steady investor can make money in the long run if they employ strategies that take advantage of upswings, diminish losses during down periods, and make some gains during sideways markets.

You have probably seen charts illustrating the potential of growing your money in the stock market. It is worth revisiting. The following charts show how much $1 invested in the DOW in 1920 and $1 invested in the S&P in 1928 would have increased.

Demonstration of Value of $1 Invested in the DOW in 1920, Bloomberg, LP

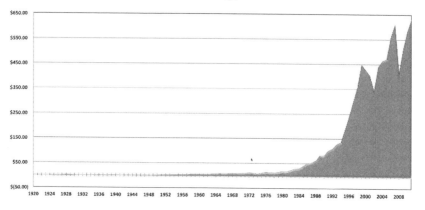

Demonstration of Value of $1 Invested in the S&P in 1928, Bloomberg, LP

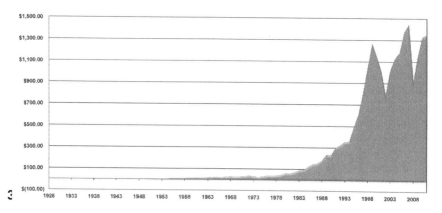

The reason these charts are worth reviewing is because they are clear evidence of the historical long–term trend of both markets. Despite great year-to-year volatility, both markets have moved upwards over the long term during the last 80–90 years.

For further illustration, let's look at the raw numbers, the year-by-year actual returns of the DOW from 1920–2014 and the S&P from 1928–2014. These numbers are instructive because they demonstrate the actual year-to-year swings in both markets.

Note how random the numbers are. Some periods can be tied to historical events: negative years around the Great Depression and positive years around the Dot.Com Boom. Yet there is no discernible pattern in the year-to-year fluctuations. Even if you could detect a pattern, it would make no difference in determining future projections.

Dow Jones Industrial Annual Returns: 1920-2016: Source: Bloomberg, LP

Year	Return	Year	Return	Year	Return
1920	(32.9)	1951	14.4	1981	(-3.6)
1921	12.3	1952	8.4	1982	27.1
1922	21.5	1953	(-3.8)	1983	26.0
1923	(-2.7)	1954	44.0	1984	1.3
1924	26.1	1955	20.8	1985	33.6
1925	30	1956	2.3	1986	27.1
1926	0.3	1957	(-12.7)	1987	5.5
1927	27.7	1958	34.0	1988	16.1
1928	49.5	1959	16.4	1989	32.2
1929	(-17.2)	1960	(-9.3)	1990	(-0.6)
1930	(-33.8)	1961	18.7	1991	24.1
1931	(-52.7)	1962	(-10.8)	1992	7.4
1932	(-22.6)	1963	20.8	1993	17.0
1933	63.7	1964	18.8	1994	5.0
1934	5.4	1965	14.4	1995	36.9
1935	38.5	1966	(-16.0)	1996	28.9
1936	24.8	1967	19.2	1997	24.9
1937	(-32.8)	1968	7.9	1998	18.1
1938	27.7	1969	(-11.8)	1999	27.2

Year	Return	Year	Return	Year	Return
1939	(-2.8)	1970	9.2	2000	(-4.7)
1940	(12.6)	1971	9.3	2001	(-5.4)
1941	(-15.4)	1972	18.5	2002	(-15)
1942	7.6	1973	(-13.3)	2003	28.3
1943	13.6	1974	(-23.6)	2004	5.3
1944	11.82	1975	44.8	2005	1.8
1945	26.9	1976	22.8	2006	19
1946	(-8.1)	1977	(-12.8)	2007	8.9
1947	2.2	1978	2.7	2008	(-31.9)
1948	(-2.1)	1979	10.5	2009	22.7
1949	13.1	1980	22.2	2010	14
1950	17.4			2011	8.4
				2012	8.84
				2013	29.65
				2014	10.04
				2015	0.21
				2016	16.50

S&P 500 Annual Returns 1928-2016
Source: Bloomberg, LP

Year	Return	Year	Return	Year	Return
1928	37.9	1957	(-10.7)	1986	18.7
1929	(-11.9)	1958	43.1	1987	5.3
1930	(-28.5)	1959	11.9	1988	16.6
1931	(-47.1)	1960	0.5	1989	31.7
1932	(-14.8)	1961	26.9	1990	(-3.1)
1933	44.1	1962	(-8.7)	1991	30.5
1934	(-4.7)	1963	22.7	1992	7.6
1935	41.4	1964	16.4	1993	10.1
1936	33.7	1965	12.4	1994	1.3
1937	(-34.7)	1966	(-10)	1995	37.6
1938	30.1	1967	23.9	1996	23
1939	(-0.1)	1968	11	1997	33.4
1940	(-9.6)	1969	(-8.4)	1998	28.6

Year	Return	Year	Return	Year	Return
1941	(-11.6)	1970	3.8	1999	21
1942	20.1	1971	14.3	2000	(-9.2)
1943	25.6	1972	19.2	2001	(-12)
1944	19.5	1973	(-14.3)	2002	(-22.1)
1945	36.3	1974	(-26.5)	2003	28.7
1946	(-8)	1975	37.2	2004	10.9
1947	5.6	1976	23.9	2005	4.9
1948	5.4	1977	(-7.2)	2006	15.8
1949	23.6	1978	6.6	2007	5.5
1950	32.6	1979	18.6	2008	(-37)
1951	23.8	1980	32.5	2009	26.5
1952	18.2	1981	(-4.9)	2010	15
1953	(-0.9)	1982	21.5	2011	2.1
1954	52.3	1983	22.6	2012	16
1955	31.4	1984	6.2	2013	32.39
1956	6.5	1985	31.7	2014	13.69
				2015	1.38
				2016	11.96

The preceding charts demonstrate the past annual volatility of returns for the DOW and S&P. The long-term upward trend is not as apparent here, but the year-to-year fluctuations in both markets should be clear. These charts are very important, and we will refer to them throughout this analysis.

Up Markets Defined

It stands to reason that it should be easy to maximize investments and accumulate wealth during an *up* market period—but how do you define an *up* market? Also, would you recognize an *up* market in time to take advantage of it? If we define an *up* market as a five-year period during which the S&P continued to rise for five consecutive years, or at least four out of five years, you would find this occurred relatively frequently:

UP Periods in the S&P: Bloomberg, LP

1941-45 (4-1)	1959-63 (4-1)	1986-90 (4-1)
1942-46 (4-1)	1960-64 (4-1)	1987-91 (4-1)
1943-47 (4-1)	1961-65 (4-1)	1988-92 (4-1)
1944-48 (4-1)	1963-67 (4-1)	1989-93 (4-1)
1945-49 (4-1)	1964-68 (4-1)	1990-94 (4-1)
1946-50 (4-1)	1967-71 (4-1)	1991-95 (5-0)
1947-51 (5-0)	1968-72 (4-1)	1992-96 (5-0)
1948-52 (5-0)	1975-79 (4-1)	1993-97 (5-0)
1949-53 (4-1)	1976-80 (4-1)	1994-98 (5-0)
1950-54 (4-1)	1978-82 (4-1)	1995-99 (5-0)
1951-55 (4-1)	1979-83 (4-1)	1996-2000 (4-1)
1952-56 (4-1)	1980-84 (4-1)	2002-06 (4-1)
1954-58 (4-1)	1981-85 (4-1)	2003-07 (5-0)
1955-59 (4-1)	1982-86 (5-0)	2004-08 (4-1)
1956-60 (4-1)	1983-87 (5-0)	2005-09 (4-1)
1957-61 (4-1)	1984-88 (5-0)	2006-10 (4-1)
1958-62 (4-1)	1985-89 (5-0)	2007-11 (4-1)
		2008-12 (4-1)
		2009-13 (5-0)
		2010-14 (5-0)
		2011-2015 (5-0)
		2012-2016 (5-0)

The preceding charts show that roughly 60 percent of the five-year periods have been *up* according to our definition. However, an up period does not guarantee an investor positive returns. It only takes one severe down year to wipe out four years of positive gains. Also, if you buy high during an *up* period, you could do further damage to your portfolio when the market levels.

Look at the S&P since 2000. There were only four years with negative returns—all the other years were positive. There was only one negative since 2003, but 2008 was so severe that the S&P was down nearly 40 percent. Many investors saw gains made during the nice run of positive years from 2003 through 2007 disappear in 2008. Thus, building wealth—even in up periods—can be tricky without a long–term investment strategy.

Boom Period (1982-1999): An Anomaly?

If you look at the preceding charts, you will see that the years 1982 through 1999 saw a historic run in the S&P—showing positive returns in 17 out of 18 years. The lone down year came in 1990.

Given the 80-plus years of S&P data, this long period of consistent positive returns is seemingly an anomaly. There are no other comparable periods, or anything even close to it. Part of the explanation might be simple supply–demand of securities. During this period, the entire Baby Boomer generation was in saving and investing mode. The youngest Boomers (those born in 1964), ages 18–35, were just beginning to save and invest. The oldest Boomers (those born in 1946), ages 36–53, were not yet in retirement liquidation mode. Certainly, other factors, such as the end of the Cold War, the Internet revolution, and interest rates and fiscal policy, played an important role in the period as well.

Regardless of the reasons, if we back out the anomalous years, the impact is notable. There were 65 positive years out of the 87 between 1928 through 2016—over 70 percent. If you take out the 18–year boom period, the percentage of positive years dips to 65 percent.

How do you take advantage of these periods?

How to Build Wealth in *Up* Markets

If you suddenly found yourself in the middle of an *up* market, seemingly all you would need to do is blindly throw a dart at a list of stocks and watch the money roll in. It is not that easy. Despite consistent *up* periods, many investors' returns have been negative or flat for the past decade. This is often due to two factors:

1. Attempted Market timing—as discussed above, and in greater detail in Lesson Six.

2. Significant down years: 2002 and 2008 were two of the worst years in either index since the Great Depression. Without downside protection, gains made in positive years can be wiped out in market slides.

Given these challenges, how does one build wealth in up markets?

Diversification: The Golden Rule

We are strong proponents of Diversification—or the practice of not putting all your eggs in one basket. We believe the best and most time-tested method for protection of investment assets is diversification.

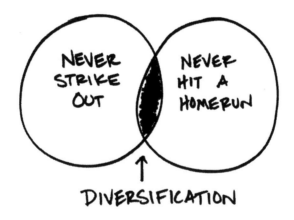

DIVERSIFICATION

Diversification through asset allocation among different types of investment options, and further diversification within these asset classes, is the hallmark of any successful portfolio. A truly diversified investment portfolio attempts to maintain the best possible expected level of return in relation to its level of acceptable risk. Modern Portfolio Theory is based on this simply described, yet complex to implement, concept.

Looking at the big picture and comparing six asset classes—large stocks, small stocks, long term government bonds, international stocks, treasury bills, and diversified portfolios—you will see that diversified portfolios were the most consistent performers, with all other classes showing great year-to-year volatility. The following chart shows different asset class winners from year to year, 1997–2016:

Asset-Class Winners and Losers 2002-2016

	2002	2003	2004	2005	2006	2007	2008	2009	2010	2011	2012	2013	2014	2015	2016	15-Year Return
Best	Fixed Income 10.3%	EM Stocks 55.8%	EM Stocks 25.6%	EM Stocks 34.0%	EM Stocks 32.1%	EM Stocks 39.4%	Fixed Income 5.2%	EM Stocks 78.5%	US Small Stocks 26.9%	Fixed Income 7.8%	EM Stocks 18.2%	US Small Stocks 38.8%	US Large Stocks 13.7%	US Large Stocks 1.4%	US Small Stocks 21.3%	EM Stocks 9.5%
	EM Stocks -6.2%	US Small Stocks 47.3%	Dev Intl Stocks 20.2%	Dev Intl Stocks 13.5%	Dev Intl Stocks 26.3%	Global Stocks 11.7%	Balanced Portfolio -22.8%	Global Stocks 34.6%	EM Stocks 18.9%	US Large Stocks 2.1%	US Large Stocks 17.3%	Dev Intl Stocks 32.4%	Balanced Portfolio 6.0%	Fixed Income 0.5%	US Large Stocks 12.0%	US Small Stocks 8.5%
	Balanced Portfolio -9.4%	Dev Intl Stocks 38.6%	US Small Stocks 18.3%	Global Stocks 10.8%	Global Stocks 21.0%	Dev Intl Stocks 11.2%	US Small Stocks -33.8%	Dev Intl Stocks 31.8%	US Large Stocks 15.1%	Balanced Portfolio 1.9%	US Small Stocks 16.3%	Global Stocks 22.8%	Fixed Income 6.0%	Dev Intl Stocks -0.8%	EM Stocks 11.2%	US Large Stocks 6.7%
	Dev Intl Stocks -15.9%	Global Stocks 34.0%	Global Stocks 15.2%	Balanced Portfolio 5.2%	US Small Stocks 18.4%	Fixed Income 7.0%	US Large Stocks -37.0%	US Small Stocks 27.2%	Global Stocks 12.7%	US Small Stocks -4.2%	Global Stocks 16.1%	Dev Intl Stocks 22.8%	US Stocks 4.9%	Balanced Portfolio -1.5%	Global Stocks 7.9%	Global Stocks 5.9%
	Global Stocks -19.3%	US Large Stocks 28.7%	US Large Stocks 10.9%	US Large Stocks 4.9%	US Large Stocks 15.8%	Balanced Portfolio 6.8%	Global Stocks -42.2%	US Large Stocks 26.5%	Balanced Portfolio 12.6%	Global Stocks -7.3%	US Large Stocks 16.0%	Balanced Portfolio 12.1%	Global Stocks 4.2%	Global Stocks -2.4%	Balanced Portfolio 7.8%	Balanced Portfolio 5.7%
	US Small Stocks -20.5%	Balanced Portfolio 21.0%	Balanced Portfolio 9.9%	US Small Stocks 4.6%	Balanced Portfolio 12.5%	US Large Stocks 5.5%	Dev Intl Stocks -43.4%	Balanced Portfolio 19.9%	Dev Intl Stocks 7.8%	Dev Intl Stocks -12.1%	Balanced Portfolio 12.1%	Fixed Income -2.0%	EM Stocks -2.2%	US Small Stocks -4.4%	Fixed Income 2.6%	Dev Intl Stocks 5.3%
Worst	US Large Stocks -22.1%	Fixed Income 4.1%	Fixed Income 4.3%	Fixed Income 2.4%	Fixed Income 4.3%	US Small Stocks -1.6%	EM Stocks -53.3%	Fixed Income 5.9%	Fixed Income 6.5%	EM Stocks -18.4%	Fixed Income 4.2%	EM Stocks -2.6%	Dev Intl Stocks -4.9%	EM Stocks -14.9%	Dev Intl Stocks 1.0%	Fixed Income 4.6%

See appendix for magnified chart

As the above chart demonstrates, yesterday's high–performing asset class can easily become tomorrow's loser. Even in positive markets, diversification is the golden rule—better performance with less risk. No matter how diversified you are in the equities markets, if you are committing all your resources to the equities market, you are not truly diversified. While you may have hedged against some level of risk, you have not hedged against the risk of the entire market decline. Again—this bolsters the argument in favor of a holistic Financial Planning Process that evolves with you as you progress through differing stages of your life.

What We Learned about Diversification in 2008

Prior to 2008, proper diversification meant allocating among the major assets classes listed above—large cap, small cap, international, bonds, etc. However, this version of diversification was problematic because these major asset classes were strongly correlated. Many investors realized that this version of diversification was ineffective during major down swings that affected the entire equities market. Let's look at the asset classes' performance in 2008.

1. Fixed Income = 5.2 percent

2. Balanced Portfolio = -22.8 percent

3. U.S. Small Stocks = -33.8 percent

4. U.S. Large Stocks = -37 percent

5. Global Stocks = -42.2 percent

6. Developed International Stocks = -43.4

7. Emerging Markets = -53.3

The other alleged *safe haven* for stock market diversification many investors rely on is real estate. Yet property values fell equally hard in 2008. The S&P/Case–Shiller Home Price Indices (Case–Shiller) is the leading measure for the U.S. residential housing market. Case–Shiller reported its largest drop in history, 18.2 percent in 2008. Thus, real estate as a stock market hedge simply did not work.

Other investors dabbled in hedge funds as a diversification tool, but they learned the hard way that many flash-in-the-pan hedge fund managers popularized with big gains in the early years of managing their fund rarely, if ever, maintain that momentum. Strong hedge fund performers attracted many investors in the late 1990s. Unfortunately, the majority of these funds took a beating in 2008. The average hedge fund performance that year was a loss of 23 percent—not much of a hedge.

The best advisors advocate fundamental, long-term investing that utilizes a portfolio customized according to the investor's risk tolerance, time horizon and tax considerations. Asset allocation drives the portfolio construction because a properly diversified portfolio can generally provide greater returns with less risk. Allocation cannot alleviate all risk—it simply spreads out the risk. However, a diversified portfolio is still susceptible to systematic event that causes the entire market to decrease.

Down Markets (and the Nikkei Review)

As you have seen in the above charts, negative market years have thus far been relatively rare in comparison with positive years. Historically, there have been few periods of consecutive negative years in the U.S. markets.

Still, a single negative market year can wipe out gains accumulated over many consecutive positive periods. The objective in getting through these periods is to mitigate losses so they do not wipe out all the gains made during rising markets.

Down Market Periods Defined

If we define a *down* market the same way we defined *up* markets above—five consecutive years of negative returns, or four out of five years with negative returns—you will see that markets historically rarely go down for a long period without at least a few up years.

Down Periods for the S&P: Bloomberg, LP

1928-32 (1-4)	1929-33 (1-4)	1930-34 (1-4)	1937-41 (1-4)

Note: There has not been a single five-year period in the history of the S&P with five straight years of negative returns.

Most people with a passing knowledge of American history have heard the stories about the Great Depression. Would it surprise you to learn that between the years of 1929 and 1940, the S&P posted three years with positive returns? Markets still experienced positive years, even during the worst economic crisis in history.

What should also jump out from the information above is that long-term *down* markets have been rare in the U.S. That is not to say they may not happen more frequently in the future, but history demonstrates that the market *has rarely been down for more than two straight years*

Years of Consecutive Down Periods in the S&P: Bloomberg, LP

1929-1932	4 years
1939-1941	3 years
1973-1974	2 years
2000-2002	3 years

Going Forward

Despite the data above, many investors now believe that the U.S. market is moving in a different direction. We should not just look to *our* past to understand how markets may work in the future. The U.S. might look more like other countries that have experienced long–term steep declines in their stock markets.

In order to examine the possibility of a long–term decline in the U.S. securities market, we will examine the most prominent stock market decline of a major global industrialized nation: the decline of Japan's Nikkei 225 stock market since the early 1990s.

Case Study: Going Abroad—The Nikkei

The Nikkei is the broad stock market for the Japanese economy, similar to the DOW. Many powerhouse companies are listed on the Nikkei, including Sony, Toyota, Honda, and Mitsubishi. The Nikkei had a tremendous 20–year run from 1970 through 1990. It was volatile during this time frame, but it was mostly upward volatility, as the chart below clearly shows:

NIKKEI from 1970 through 2011: Bloomberg, LP

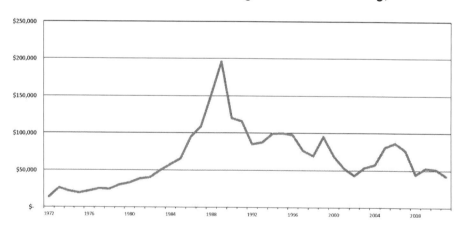

See appendix for magnified chart

However, as you can see, starting in 1990 and continuing through today, the Nikkei lost more than 60 percent of its value. The index peaked in December of 1989 at 38,916, and by December of 2011, it had declined to 8,458. As we discussed, markets in the U.S. have not experienced any similar long–term market declines, but as the Nikkei shows, it's possible.

Note: During this precipitous decline, there were still no *down* periods of five-out-of-five, or even four-out-of-five down years during a single five-year-period. Also, consider how many positive years there were, even in the Nikkei's historic down market. Even though it decreased by 60 percent in value from 1990–2011, there were still many positive years mixed in as the market slid. In fact, nearly half of the years were positive—nine out of those 20 years! See below:

NIKKEI Returns 1991-2010. Source: Bloomberg, LP

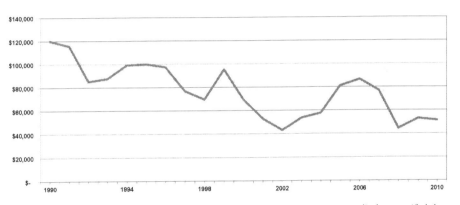

See appendix for magnified chart

1991	(-3.63)	9,637
1992	(-26.36)	7,097
1993	2.91	7,303
1994	13.24	8,270
1995	0.74	8,331
1996	(-2.55)	8,118
1997	(-21.19)	6,398
1998	(-9.28)	5,804
1999	36.79	7,939
2000	(-27.19)	5,780
2001	(-23.52)	4,421
2002	(-18.63)	3,597

2003	24.45	4,477
2004	7.61	4,817
2005	40.24	6,756
2006	6.92	7,223
2007	(-11.13)	6,419
2008	(-42.12)	3,715
2009	19.04	4,422
2010	(-3.01)	4,289

Not only were there nine positive years, but many of those years were up significantly. There were huge positive years where surely some investors in the Nikkei were able to take advantage of the market. In fact, there was even an *up* market within our definition above during this down trend, four straight positive years (2003–2006) in the middle of one of the most historic down trends of one of the world's largest stock markets.

Even if we assume that the U.S. markets could be in for a multi–year negative decline (something they have never experienced before), and if Japan is a model for such a decline, then we could expect the period to include many *positive* years.

Can You Make Money in Short-Term Down Markets? Is it Worth the Risk?

Obviously, it is difficult to make money when the markets are showing negative returns. If individual stocks, asset classes, and global markets are all declining, how do investors make money?

Shorting is one trading technique investors have used for decades to take advantage of down markets. When an investor goes *short* on a security, they are anticipating a decrease in the share price. The investor borrows funds from a third party with the intent of buying the security back at a later date. The investor is attempting to sell something high *now*, and buy it back at a lower price *later*. The investor is betting against the security and profiting from the anticipated decline in the security's price.

The short seller will incur a loss if the price of the security rises, since the investor will have to buy the securities back at a higher price than they sold them (a short seller's loss potential is technically unlimited as a stock price in theory can go to infinity). There are also other costs of shorting, including fees for borrowing the assets and payment of any dividends paid on the borrowed assets. By definition, *shorting* is not a long–term investment strategy. Shorting is a trading technique sometimes attempted to make a gain when a security or market is trending down over the short term. Shorting is essentially another way to try to time the market.

Is it worth the risk?

It is extremely difficult to build wealth in down market periods without taking on larger risk. Techniques like shorting may generate gains, but they are risky and not considered long–term investment strategies. The key to long–term successful investing is to not lose too much in down periods. Limiting your downside is crucial—to illustrate the importance of downside protection, we look to simple algebra to illustrate. Many folks fail to realize that if your portfolio incurs a 50 percent loss, it does not take that same 50 percent gain to get the value back to even, rather it would take a 100 percent gain to recoup your losses. What if you experienced a 20 percent loss...wouldn't it take a 40 percent return to get back to even? Not quite as a 20 percent loss would only need a 25 percent gain to get back to your original portfolio value.

The main goal in a long-term investment plan is to avoid huge losses during down periods. The planning will likely not yield gains during bad times, but it will help avoid wiping out gains made during good times.

Historically, there have not been long-term declines in the U.S. markets since the 1920s. Even in the Nikkei's severe down trend, there were many significant upswings dotting the landscape. Wise investors do not panic in down markets, and some have found ways to take advantage of upticks by following long-term investment strategies.

Sideways Markets

We have looked at *up* markets (bulls) and *down* markets (bears), and how historically *up* markets have been far more common than *down* markets. What about the common *sideways* market? How do you accumulate and sustain wealth when the market is flat?

Sideways Markets Defined: a five-year period wherein there are at least two years with positive returns and at least two years with negative returns. These are important market periods to understand because they have occurred relatively frequently.

Many investment advisors discuss *ad nauseam* the gains they made during positive markets and how they beat the market during negative market periods. However, these same advisors usually ignore the frequent *sideways* markets. The best long-term investment strategies should attempt to account for all market conditions.

For the last 80-plus years, the U.S. stock market has inched along with periods of growth followed by years of decline—wash, rinse, repeat. See the S&P:

Sideways Periods in the S&P 500: Bloomberg, LP

1931-35 (2-3)	1953-57 (3-2)	1974-78 (3-2)
1932-36 (3-2)	1962-66 (3-2)	1977-81 (3-2)
1933-37 (3-2)	1965-69 (3-2)	1997-2001 (3-2)
1934-38 (3-2)	1966-70 (3-2)	1998-02 (2-3)
1935-39 (3-2)	1969-73 (3-2)	1999-03 (2-3)
1936-40 (2-3)	1970-74 (3-2)	2000-04 (2-3)
1938-42 (3-2)	1971-75 (3-2)	2001-05 (3-2)
1939-43 (2-3)	1972-76 (3-2)	
1940-44 (3-2)	1973-77 (3-2)	

Over 30 percent of the five-year periods in the S&P were sideways. If you take out the 1982–1999 anomaly period, then sideways periods jump to 38 percent of the S&P. Given this significant percentage of time, it makes sense that if you cannot make gains during *sideways* markets, you simply cannot build wealth.

What Does This Mean for Investing?

Let's take a hypothetical 11-year time period wherein every year it switches up, then down by the same incremental amount: year one up ten percent, year two down ten percent, year three up, year four down, and so on. You would assume that at the very least you would break even. However, as you will see, if you do nothing to mitigate the losses taken in the down years, you will not gain and you will not break even. You will actually lose money over time.

The assumption of the average investor is that if the market is up as often as it is down and if all the swings are equal, then we should at least break even. That assumption is incorrect, and we will show you why, starting with $1,000:

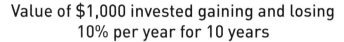

Value of $1,000 invested gaining and losing 10% per year for 10 years

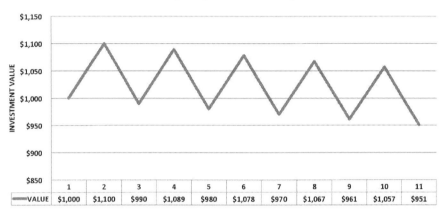

	1	2	3	4	5	6	7	8	9	10	11
VALUE	$1,000	$1,100	$990	$1,089	$980	$1,078	$970	$1,067	$961	$1,057	$951

Have you spotted the trend? The $1,000 you started with would eventually turn into $951. Your average rate of return would be zero, but your actual rate of return would be –4.9 percent.

Even if you were lucky enough to pull your investment during a positive year, your initial investment did little to grow. Rather, it bounced back and forth—up one year, down the next. And, of course, this hypothetical market did not include expenses, like investment manager fees or taxes. So how does an investor make money in a *sideways* market?

Making Money in *Sideways* Markets

As discussed above, a well-balanced, properly allocated portfolio wherein tax-drag is accounted for regularly should perform well over the long run even in sideways markets. Allocation goes beyond diversified securities. It extends to investments that are not correlated to the U.S. Equity Market. Typically, these non-correlated vehicles include hedge funds, private equity, private debt, private real estate investment trusts (REITs), structured products, etc.

Big Picture: What Does This *All* Mean?

As the information above shows, markets are wildly unpredictable. We hope you will keep this information in mind as we discuss in the following Lessons on different strategies for managing your wealth.

In our opinion, the best way to navigate unpredictable elements is to chart a course and stick to it, but remain flexible to avoid getting trapped. You must adjust at times—but adjust strategically, rather than emotionally. You will likely need help—but where do you get the help you can trust that makes sense for your specific circumstances? We cover the answers to these questions in the following Lessons.

Experience makes experts of us all—but you can't get experience overnight. However, if you understand the history, you gain experience a little quicker and much less painlessly.

As the data above demonstrates; the long-play is the safest and best play. Patience will help you navigate the playing field and avoid repeating past mistakes that have doomed other investors. Be *smart* and learn from your mistakes—but also be *wise* and learn from the mistakes of others.

How Do I Find the Right Advisor (or Do I even *Need* an Advisor)?

"Constantly probe the people who report to you, and encourage them to probe you."

—Ray Dalio, investor, hedge fund manager and philanthropist

In Part II, we will answer common questions we have heard from people over the years:

Do I really need help—or can I handle wealth management on my own?

How can I find the right professional to work with?

What are my options?

How can I tell how my advisors are doing?

These are common questions that many investors are anxious to ask. In Part II; we provide you some answers and guidance to make it easier for you to decide what you need to do next. Surround yourself with the right people and make sure they are willing to advise you and answer all your questions.

Understand Your Options
for Wealth Management Advice

*"Knowing what you don't know
is more useful than being brilliant."*

–Charlie Munger,
Warren Buffett's partner at Berkshire Hathaway

In today's 24-hour news cycle and endless streams of social media, it can become very difficult to filter through the noise. That noise can be suffocating for investors who are simply trying to work hard and save for their future. That future is dependent upon many variables and some of them are very much out of your control. Life events happen and can change the trajectory of even the best-laid plans.

What you can control is taking steps to put a plan in place to manage your wealth. Whether you seek professional advice for your financial future or you prefer to go it alone—you must have a plan (see Part III).

Maybe your idea of wealth management is a plan where you make more, spend less and retire before reaching 60 years old. This is a plan—still vague, but now there is at least a timeline and target. However, this plan is still missing important pieces. How much is enough to retire? What assumptions on growth and inflation have you used? How can you protect what you have saved so far? How can you put your savings to work for you? And, it is still missing any meaningful guidance along the way.

The first place to start for anyone—is to determine *if* they need help; and if so, how to choose the right advisor (or if they even need an advisor). This Lesson outlines the many options to choose from.

What are your options?

The most common options for managing your wealth are below. There are subcategories, but here we just wanted to provide a general snapshot. We believe the decision of who you trust your wealth management to will be one of the most important financial decisions you will ever make. Whether you choose to do-it-yourself, or hire a professional advisor—you must understand the ramifications of your decision.

Do-it-yourself

Some people recognize the need for finding help with their holistic planning, but may believe they can still handle their investments on their own.

Definition: An individual investor who builds a portfolio and selects their own individual investments without the assistance of a professional advisor.

Why would one choose to do it yourself? To reduce expenses and self-educate.

Reducing fees is nothing to scoff at—fee drag can make a difference on overall performance of your investments. It is imperative that, if you choose an advisor, you understand how they are compensated and how this will affect your planning.

Some people have a passion for investing—most of these people go into professional advisory services, research or teaching. That said, we have met many people with vocations outside of the profession who love researching investments and setting their own plans—managing their wealth. It is close to a full-time pursuit. For people who do it successfully, they generally dedicate as much time to it as others dedicate to golfing or other hobbies.

It is possible to manage your own wealth and achieve success in the long run; but in most cases, we find that the typical *DIY'ers* are prone to bias, inconsistent attention and other obstacles that hinder their long-term success. See Lesson Six for more on these potential obstacles.

Why not do it yourself? There are many reasons, we will focus on the most common.

- It takes time, and there is an opportunity cost of professional time. Every hour spent researching stocks, evaluating portfolio risk, trading, waiting on hold to speak with your discount broker, communicating with your tax advisor or attorney regarding your investments, is time you are not generating revenue or spending time living, doing the activities you love, spending time with your family, etc.

- A professional advisor has access to the best technology and the benefit of scalability; a do-it-yourselfer does not. DIY'ers are generally locked out of most private equity, real estate investment trusts (detailed below) and other ancillary investment opportunities. This may be okay for many who have no interest in these more sophisticated investment opportunities.

- Money is emotional. If you are like most affluent investors, losses become more impactful as your wealth increases. Objectivity is very difficult. Accepting paper losses is a part of investing. Every investor has their breaking point or loss threshold. Recognizing a loss threshold prior to investing is important. The ability to stick to your threshold is very difficult and typically requires the support of a professional (see Lesson Six).

Learning to invest *via* self-education can be costly. Financial markets are dynamic and constantly evolving. New products are brought to the market every year. Central banks introduced unprecedented measures of stimulus in the last decade. Transparency within the financial industry is improving, yet not where it should be to help the individual investor. Every investor is going to make mistakes, including the professionals. Learning from mistakes and being able to minimize the impact of those mishaps, can be the difference between a successful and a failed plan.

Doing it yourself can be a great strategy for some clients for at least part of their portfolio. It can give you the opportunity to learn about your investments as you begin to build your portfolio, becoming an engaged investor. It will allow you to understand how markets work, begin to familiarize yourself with your tolerance for volatility and risk, and most importantly, become familiar with the various investments/products that are available in the marketplace.

Aside from some of the educational benefits of do-it-yourself investing, there are some actual economic benefits as well.

Typically, a do-it-yourself investor will have one of the lowest cost ways to invest in the markets. You will not have to pay commissions or advisory fees, but you will be subject to the internal costs of the funds that you purchase as well as any transactional costs at your custodian. Any time you can remove fees and keep the total cost of your portfolio as low as possible, you will help drive long-term performance.

The most successful do-it-yourself investors are extremely disciplined, have ample time to study the markets and, in our opinion, must thoroughly enjoy the process of managing their assets. The last point is of utmost importance. We have found that clients who choose the do-it-yourself method of investing simply to save advisory fees, but lack the time and the overall enjoyment of the research process of investing, become frustrated and dissatisfied with the markets as a whole.

Theoretically, no one has a greater interest than you in protecting and looking after your investments. However, your personal interest in protecting and looking after your investments may be the single greatest factor working *against* your investment performance. Most investors are risk-averse, biased creatures prone to putting too much credence into noise, trends and herd mentality. In the legal field, there is an old saying (often attributed to Abraham Lincoln): "an attorney who represents himself has a fool for a client." Does this adage also apply to finance? In many cases, it does.

Why do individual investors do so poorly? You have likely heard of the impact of the basic human emotions of *greed* and *fear* on investing—getting overly optimistic when the market goes up, assuming it will continue to do so, and wanting in on the action (GREED) and becoming extremely pessimistic during downturns and wanting out before losing everything (FEAR)— for more on this, *see* Lesson Six.

Because they do not have an interest in investing, the time to dedicate to it, or because they would rather spend any time they do have in more productive or fulfilling activities, most investors work with a professional investment advisor. Beyond these personal concerns, there are also some studies that suggest that there is significant value in working with an investment advisor over time. Let's examine two such studies—one that focuses specifically on the value of an investment advisor and another which focuses on the value of an advisor in comprehensive wealth management.

The Value of an Advisor

A recent Vanguard study[1] stated "(t)he value proposition for advisors has always been easier to describe than to define." Why is quantifying the actual value of advisory services so difficult? Because value is subjective and the perceived and actual value of wealth management advice will vary from person to person.

That said, we spend significant time with our clients (and in Lesson Six) reviewing the components of wealth management that can be objectively quantified—based on certain conditions. We can only estimate the value of each piece of wealth management because each piece will be implemented differently, for different reasons, for each individual—and each piece will further react differently based on economic and market environments.

Every advisor charges something for their advice. It may be tempting to create a *cost-benefit analysis* to attempt to produce an annualized figure that clearly defines the advisor's actual value or the value of the tools they implement for you. But this, again, is very difficult because the value may not be consistent year-to-year, but more sporadic. Further, the value may be not in what is executed and/or implemented—but rather *in what is* avoided during mania and panic and when greed and fear tempt you to deviate from your course. On an individual basis, any attempt would be riddled with unprovable assumptions.

The Vanguard study did attempt this analysis, though, in general, across the population and with big data—to quantify the value-add of certain best practices in investing. They looked specifically at the following:

---

[1] *"Putting a Value On Your Value: Quantifying Vanguard Advisor's Alpha*; (September 2016) Vanguard Research; accessed on March 15, 2017 via url: https://www.vanguard.com/pdf/ISGQVAA.pdf.

- Appropriate asset allocation/diversification (discussed further in Lessons Two and Six)

- Cost effective implementation—i.e. taking into account all fees and costs concerning your investments (see more in Lessons Three, Four, Five and Six)

- Rebalancing

- Behavioral coaching (see Lesson Six)

- Asset location/utilizing different accounts efficiently (see Lesson Seven)

- Spending strategy and withdrawal order (see Lesson Four)

- Total return versus income investing[2]

As with most things—the value is in the whole, rather than the sum of your wealth management's parts. The value is difficult to discern at a granular level and rarely reveals itself in quarterly or annual statements. It is rare that advisors highlight the landmines avoided in the past but the "value and impact on clients' wealth creation is very real."[3] Taking all parts into account, Vanguard estimated advisors can potentially add 3 percent in net returns—calculated retroactively on an annual basis.

But that 3 percent claim comes with a heavy qualification—it will *vary annually* based on each person's unique circumstances and will *not be a regular, annual figure*—but rather will reveal itself over the long term.

We are not claiming that every professional advisor *will* add value to your life. No one *can* make that claim. Rather, advisors can add value if they take the time and interest in taking into account *your* entire picture and planning and managing according to your personal situation.

---

[2] Ultimately Vanguard determined that "value is deemed significant but too unique to each investor" to accurately quantify total returns versus income investing because each investor's spending, saving and portfolio composition is specific to them personally. *Id.*

[3] *Id.*

Paying for the advice and guidance of a trusted advisor can add meaningful value compared to the average investor experience. Therefore, it is helpful to know what options you have; what questions to ask and how best to work with the advisor you choose. Let's examine these options and questions below.

Quantified Value of Professional Guidance

An additional Morningstar study[4] sought to "define the additional value achieved by an individual investor from making more intelligent financial planning decisions" with the aid of professional advice. They focused on retirees who received comprehensive wealth management advice including assistance with strategies that consider customized withdrawal plans during retirement; tax efficiency; total wealth asset allocation; guaranteed income efficiency and asset allocation predicated on future spending needs.

This Morningstar study is important because it demonstrated that a retiree could expect "an annual return increase of plus 1.59 percent…a significant improvement in portfolio efficiency for a retiree."[5] The study states the "results are strong enough to highlight the difference that intelligent financial planning can make for investors."[6] The study is not an apples-to-apples comparison for all investment and wealth management planning. It focuses on income stability versus performance and reaching/exceeding specified goals.

We will go into detail about the importance of planning and holistic wealth management in Lesson Seven; but first we think it's important to spend time answering the crucial questions: "What types of advisors exist to provide wealth management advice…and how do they make money? What are the pros/cons of each? Why would an investor consider one type over another?" Let's dig into these answers now.

---

[4] *Alpha, Beta and Now…Gamma* (August 28, 2013); Morningstar Investment Management accessed on March 11, 2017 via url: http://corporate.morningstar.com/ib/documents/PublishedResearch/AlphaBetaandNowGamma.pdf.

[5] *Id*. At page 16 of 28.

[6] *Id*.

Professional Advisor Options:

1. Brokers and Banks

 If you choose to work with a professional advisor, the first choice you may think of as an investor may be a broker-dealer and/or bank-based advisor. Brokers and banks tend to be very popular because they are the largest corporations with the most marketing and, thus, why we are addressing them first.

A broker-dealer is generally a person or firm in the business of buying and selling securities, operating as both a broker and a dealer, depending on the transaction. Here are some well-known examples of such firms:

- *National/Global broker dealers* include Merrill Lynch, Morgan Stanley, or UBS.

- *Regional brokers* include firms like Raymond James and Edward Jones.

- *Bank-based advisors* are affiliated with large banks like Wells Fargo and Bank of America; they usually refer to themselves as "financial planners" and/or "financial consultants."

- *Independent broker-dealers* run their shops under their own names, but are generally affiliated with larger corporations and sells products from outside sources.

We tend to lump these types of firms into the same category because all of them share the following fundamental component— *they are not fiduciaries and are required to only abide by the suitability standard (more information below).*

Definition: A broker (also known as a registered representative) executes security trades for a commission or fee. Compensation is typically tied to the activity level in an account or is embedded within the investment products used by the financial professional. The broker or bank representative is employed by the firm holding your assets (also referred to as a "custodian"). The term "broker-dealer" is used in U.S. securities regulation parlance to describe stock brokerages, because most of them act as both agents and principals. A brokerage acts as a broker (or agent) when it executes orders on behalf of clients, whereas it acts as a dealer (or principal) when it trades for its own account.

Why would an investor use a broker: Many individuals have a perception that value is tied to activity. In a traditional commission-based environment, a client is not paying a recurring annual or quarterly fee; they are being charged for activity. It is certainly possible for a client to experience lower costs for financial advice in certain circumstances, particularly if the investor owns securities they never intend to sell. A traditional brokerage relationship is not discretionary, meaning the investor will have the ability to direct investment decisions and receive suggestions on an *ad hoc* basis.

Some of the benefits of working with some of the world's largest broker-dealers are the tremendous research capabilities, unique investment offerings and the convenience of branch offices throughout the world.

Why elect against using a bank representative or broker? The top reason is easily the conflict of interest present in a relationship where the compensation of the individual making recommendations is based on the product he or she uses for the investor. A lack of transparency in the fee-based products also means it is very difficult for an investor utilizing this type of relationship to understand what they are paying. Also, the broker's "suitability" standard is significantly weaker, from a client's perspective, than the higher "fiduciary" standard, discussed further below. Private Banking advisors also lack independence and generally seem to only use their bank's products; while *Bank Trust Departments* administer trusts under similar conflicts.

How do you know if you are working with a broker? Simply ask the advisor how they receive compensation. If you want to be more pointed with your question, ask the representative if they receive compensation from any financial products. Then follow up by asking if their employer receives compensation from financial products. An advisor should not be offended by these questions, in fact, they should welcome them. If the answer is not clear and concise, consider that to be a huge red flag.

It's important to note that most firms have realized the negative connotation that the name broker implies and have begun calling most of their sales force "financial advisors."

Another way to identify a broker is that they are employed by a firm where your assets are also held. This can create many conflicts of interest for individual investors, as there is a long history of proprietary products and incentives for the sales forces at these firms to push certain products on the clients. Remaining objective and providing a transparent business model are the biggest challenges for broker-dealers.

In our opinion, for you (the client), the superior business model has a true fiduciary working on your behalf ("fiduciary" will be defined later)—but the broker-dealer model today still uses the firm-favorable suitability standard for the relationship with their clients.

Broker's Suitability Standard

As we have referenced above, a broker has a lower standard of duty—called the "suitability standard." *This means the broker does not need to act in the best interests of the underlying customer. Instead, their actions must only must be "suitable" for the client.*

Broker-dealers are regulated by the Financial Industry Regulatory Authority (FINRA) under standards that require them to make suitable recommendations to their clients. Instead of having to place his or her interests below that of the client, the suitability standard only details that the broker-dealer has to reasonably believe that any recommendations made are suitable for clients, in terms of the client's financial needs, objectives and unique circumstances at the time of the interaction. *A key distinction in terms of loyalty is also important, in that a broker's duty is to the broker-dealer he or she works for, not necessarily the client served.*

Most brokers even today have a very convoluted fee structure for their clients. In a period of time where clients are demanding transparency and lower-cost options, you will still see sales loads on mutual funds, trading commissions, as well as many account service fees.

2. Insurance Agents
Definition: An insurance agent (also known as a "producer") typically sells a wide range of financial products. Traditional insurance

may be sold by the agent (property and casualty, life, disability, and long term care) in addition to annuities and mutual funds. We are addressing this option second because the insurance industry's marketing is nearly as pervasive as the broker-dealers and banks, so all readers should recognize them.

Many insurance agents, in fact, provide their investment advice and products through an insurance company's broker dealer. You will see many life, disability and long term care insurance agents who are also licensed to sell investments as registered representatives for the largest insurance companies brokers dealers. Examples include MassMutual Life Insurance (MML Investor Services), Northwestern Mutual (NM Investment Services), Lincoln Investment and TransAmerica Financial.

Why would an investor use an insurance agent for investments?

Typically, the first financial relationship an individual develops in their lifetime is with an insurance agent *via* auto, life or disability insurance. Once a client begins to accumulate net worth, they may consider the agent to be a comprehensive financial expert and seek advice from the agent. The idea of a single individual handling all financial affairs may be attractive to a new investor.

Why elect against using an insurance agent for investments?

Cost and a lack of transparency are the top reasons. Conflicts are inherent in the compensation structure for insurance agents. Insurance agents do not spend their time managing money, or following the markets and economy. The agents are selling insurance, consequently investment management is being outsourced. Once investments are outsourced, you are adding layers of fees.

Some insurance agents will be licensed to sell both insurance and securities/investments, including variable annuities, mutual funds, etc. They might be registered reps who can sell securities through broker-dealers like those above, but they may not necessarily be financial advisors. Moreover, if their investment advice is provided through the broker-dealer channel, the same negatives described above apply here as well, including the lack of a fiduciary duty to clients.

Insurance sales reps sell products and get commissions on those sales, which is how they are compensated. As above, they are *not* fiduciaries and do not have to function in *your* best interests.

People calling themselves "financial advisors" can run the gamut of services provided and compensation; that's why there is so much confusion on the part of clients. Insurance sales representatives and agents owe a duty to their employer, not to you—so they cannot present themselves as fiduciaries.

3. Fee-Only Financial Planners

Definition: A *fee-only planner* usually provides services for a set hourly fee ($200-$500 per hour); or for an annual retainer ($1,500-10,000).

Why would an investor use a fee-only planner? They are generally conflict-free fiduciaries. They also have a simple hourly or retainer fee structure. The cost and the fact that they will work in your best interests means you can certainly pick worse options.

Why elect against using a fee-only planner? They have their short-comings. Most fee-only planners are small shops will little in the way of resources. It's a positive that you will always talk to the same person whenever you call, but this can be a problem in a long-term, business-continuity sense—would you be comfortable with your advisor retiring and sending you to a total stranger right before you retire?

They may be certified with a professional designation (like a CFP®—Certified Financial Planner®), but may not be licensed to buy/sell securities—so while they may be able to help you craft a plan; you may have to implement it yourself. They generally have fewer technological resources and may also be shut out of more complex, but possibly advantageous investments like real estate investment trusts (REITs) or other non-traded options often utilized by high net worth individuals to further diversify their wealth.

4. Automated Investment Management (Robo-Advisors)

Definition: A *Robo-Advisor* (Robo) is an online, automated algorithm-based portfolio management/investing service provided with little or no human interaction. They typically only offer portfolio management and do not get involved in more personal aspects of wealth management, such as asset protection, income tax reduction and retirement modeling.

Why would an investor use a Robo? Robos are typically low-cost, and have low account minimums. It's a good service for simple savings/retirement planning—but generally not customizable for high net worth individuals/families with complex planning needs. Robos cater to do-it-yourself clients and younger clients who are just starting to save.

Why elect against using a Robo? Planning is generally not customizable for high net worth individuals/families with complex planning needs. A Robo will not provide the opportunity for you to communicate by phone or in person to discuss your situation. A handful of Robos are experimenting with offering a team of customer service representatives. The phone representative may be able to address basic questions; however, they do not currently provide traditional financial advice, nor any sophisticated services. Robos are new to the industry and, as such, many questions remain unanswered.

Robos provide limited services like establishing the risk profile of client, selecting the appropriate asset allocation, rebalancing and managing assets tax efficiently. However, high quality investment advisors, in addition to these basic services, also provide fully customizable, sophisticated strategies to build and preserve wealth while reducing taxes.

These services are either beyond the scope of the Robo, or provided at an additional cost. High net worth investors benefit the most from comprehensive financial planning, or when a thread is woven through investment management, retirement planning, tax planning and education planning, asset protection, insurance planning, and estate planning. This comprehensive approach works best with several professional advisors that are experts in their disciplines. This is beyond the scope of the Robo.

Professional investment advice seeks to protect clients from making emotional decisions with their money. Robo platforms provide no advice or guidance during volatile times or sharp downturns in the market. When a client calls a Robo for help, the most they will generally get is technical support only (some robos offer some human element at a higher cost or for clients with large accounts).

Nobody knows how this technology will perform during a bear market.

Controversy surrounded one of the largest Robos on June 24, 2016. The United Kingdom shocked financial markets by voting to exit the Eurozone, an event ultimately termed "Brexit." Trading was halted by this Robo for 2.5 hours during the market selloff the following morning when the Dow Jones Industrial Average tumbled more than 600 points. Clients were not able to liquidate assets during a period of market turmoil. The Robo suggested they were performing their fiduciary duty, and referenced their customer agreement which states they reserve the right to "limit or make account access unavailable during periods of market volatility, peak demand, systems upgrades, (and) maintenance" among other reasons.[7] Investors should also note, as of the time of the event, the account agreement stated the firm is not responsible for losses tied to a service suspension.

Most of the Robo services today only allow for cash transfers and deposits and are not capable of account transfers that include established positions. This will work for many small investors who are getting started, but long-term investors will be unable to participate based on holding quality investments currently and large capital gains.

Many of the current products being offered have a multitude of limitations, including limitations on type of accounts that can be created which may not allow for asset protection or estate planning (i.e., unable to create trust accounts, accounts for LLCs or FLPs). Most importantly, are the large cash positions Robos require. These minimum cash positions can be a drag on performance. Cash requirements provide an opportunity for the robos to generate revenue from your assets that are not invested. While these costs may not be substantial, they are a hidden expense a non-astute investor may not recognize.

5. Other "Advisors"

We put "advisors" here in quotes, because most here fall closer to salespeople rather than actual advisors; but over the course of the last few years—these companies have shifted to claiming an "advisory" roles when they still usually push products versus actual wealth management.

---

[7] http://www.wsj.com/articles/robo-adviser-betterment-stokes-concern-over-brexit-trading-halt-1467403366

These include:

- *Asset Managers:* big names that hold themselves out as advisors—but again, lack independence and are generally limited to only offering products affiliated with their company.

- *Hybrid-advisors;* combinations of any of the above—further confusing duties and potential conflicts.

- *Hedge funds and Private Equity firms* (see Lesson One).

The common thread is most of these types of advisors are affiliated with a big bank and/or investment company. The companies have their individual "advisors" recommend their products and struggle with offering truly objective wealth management advice.

6. Registered Investment Advisors (RIAs)

A Registered Investment Advisor (RIA) is an advisor or firm engaged in the investment advisory business and registered either with the Securities and Exchange Commission (SEC) or state securities authorities. A Registered Investment Advisor is defined by The Investment Advisors Act of 1940 as a "person or firm that, for compensation, is engaged in the act of providing advice, making recommendations, issuing reports or furnishing analyses on securities, either directly or through publications." *An investment advisor has a fiduciary duty to his or her clients, which means that he or she has a fundamental obligation to provide suitable investment advice and always act in the clients' best interests.*

Why would an investor use an RIA? An RIA must adhere to a fiduciary standard of care laid out in the U.S. Investment Advisors Act of 1940. This standard requires RIAs to act and serve a client's best interests with the intent to eliminate, or at least to expose, all potential conflicts of interest which might incline an investment advisor—consciously or unconsciously—to render advice which was not in the best interest of the RIA's clients.

The following illustration is helpful. Note that for a fiduciary, the client is at the center of the relationship. All advice must be in the client's best interest. However, for an advisor who must satisfy only the suitability standard, the product is at the center. It does not matter whether the product fits or procurement is in the client's best interest as long as the product was seemingly suitable at the time of sale and/or advice.

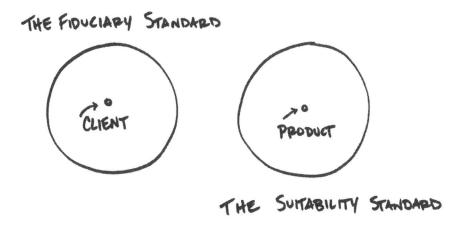

THE FIDUCIARY STANDARD

CLIENT

PRODUCT

THE SUITABILITY STANDARD

Key Benefits of Independence

Independent Registered Investment Advisors are not tied to any particular family of fund or investment products. So, whether you need help with retirement planning, a tax situation, estate planning, or managing assets at multiple places, independent advisors have the freedom to choose from a wide range of investment options in order to tailor their advice based on what's best for you.

High Level of Expertise RIAs can help investors address the variety of complex investment needs that arise when you accumulate significant wealth. While specific services vary from firm to firm, RIAs are often described as financial "quarterbacks" focused on your holistic picture. A good RIA will speak to the client in terms of his or her overall goals and objectives, and review these with the client at regular intervals.

Independent Custodians RIAs use independent custodians to hold clients' assets—including some of the world's largest custodians such as Schwab, TD, Fidelity and others. For many investors, this provides a reassuring system of checks and balances your money is not held by the same person who advises you about how to invest.

A Simple Fee Structure (Transparency) RIAs typically charge a fee based on a percentage of assets managed. This structure is simple, transparent, and easy to understand. It also gives your advisor an incentive to help grow your assets. When you succeed, your advisor succeeds.

RIAs usually earn their revenue through a management fee comprised of a percentage of assets held for a client. Fees fluctuate, but the average is around 1 to 1.5 percent. Generally, the more assets a client has, the lower the fee he or she can negotiate. This serves to align the best interests of the client with those of the RIA, as the advisor cannot make any more money on the account unless the client increases his or her asset base. All RIAs are required to include their fee schedules in their Form ADV (discussed below) filed annually with the SEC.

The most common definition of a high-net-worth investor is someone with a net worth of $1 million or more. The reason for this is that most RIA firms will establish an account minimum for anyone wishing to become a client. Amounts below this tend to be more difficult to manage while still making a profit.

Investment advisors might have a hybrid model where they sell products for commissions as well as charging fees for financial planning and investment advice, or they could be a fee-based advisor who does not sell any products (different from a fee-only/retainer arrangement discussed above). These advisors might charge a flat fee or a percentage of assets for creating financial plans, making investment recommendations, or managing money.

Advisors don't exist strictly to pick the best stock, mutual fund or ETF or to simply forecast economic conditions and make tactical decisions in a portfolio. While those are important components, an advisor should act as a buffer who puts space between you and your investments to take some of the emotion out of the decisions. An RIA can be ideally positioned, through their business model, to play this role.

Why would an investor not use an RIA? Some investors want to use a brand name, big bank or broker-dealer. Some investors understand the value of, and seek out, holistic planning—but choose to handle the investment themselves.

Conclusion

Understanding there are different options for advice is the first part of the equation. The next part is choosing the best advisor, or advisors, for *your* wealth management. The next Lesson provides questions to ask your current or prospective advisor; as well as information on how to evaluate them once you have started working with them.

Lesson Six expands the wealth management concept to discuss how your advisor needs to fit within the scope of your entire wealth management plan. We touch on the limitations of working with a single individual investment advisor versus a team of specialists.

Ask Your Advisor These Questions—and Properly Evaluate Them

"There are many ways of going forward,
but only one way of standing still."

—Franklin D. Roosevelt,
32nd President of the United States of America

Within the last 10-15 years, it seems like every consumer product or service has expanded available options. Picking an advisor is no different. Choice is a great—generally, the more options the better. However, with the advent of more choices comes increased difficulty in understanding the differences between all the options.

First, Protect Yourself and Your Wealth: Tips for Checking Out Brokers and Investment Advisors[8]

We would encourage you to consider the qualifications of anyone, regardless of what kind of advisor, you are considering working with.

- What licenses do they have?

- Do they have professional certifications?

- Are they experienced—do they handle any other specialties?

- Are they registered as a broker or advisor?

---

[8] For more questions and additional tips, you can read the SEC's publications on their website at https://www.sec.gov/index.htm. The SEC cannot recommend or endorse any particular entity, but there are a number of non-profit educational and consumer organizations that offer free tools to help investors check financial professionals.

- Do they sell products or work on a fee basis?

- Who to work with depends on what you need and want.

The following section includes information and questions to ask to help you better understand the relationship and get answers to the above questions.

Federal and/or state securities laws require investment advisors to be licensed and/or registered. Firms and advisors are also required to make important information about their profile public so you can review prior to engaging. That said, the regulatory agencies put the onus on *you* to locate information and vet the firm and advisors yourself. Luckily, the information is generally easy to locate. Before you engage any firm, make certain they have not had disciplinary problems or been in trouble with regulators or clients.

Firms and individuals who get paid to give advice about investing generally must register with either the Securities and Exchange Committee (SEC) or the state securities agency where they have their principal place of business. To find out if your advisor (or an advisor you are reviewing) is properly registered, you can view their most recent Form ADV online by visiting the Investment Advisor Public Disclosure (IAPD) website at: http://www.adviserinfo. sec.gov/. You should also be able to obtain copies from the investment advisor.

Form ADV includes two parts. Part 1 contains basic information about the advisor's business and whether they have had problems with regulators or clients. Part 2 sets out the minimum requirements for a written disclosure statement, commonly referred to as the Disclosure Brochure. Advisors must provide the Disclosure Brochure to clients. The Brochure describes the advisory firm's business practices, fee schedules, any existing conflicts of interest, and disciplinary information. Before you hire an investment advisor make sure you carefully review both parts of the Form ADV—and ask questions.

Each brochure provided must also be accompanied by a Brochure Supplement that includes information about the specific individual advisors that will act on behalf of the firm. This Supplement contains information about the individuals who will actually provide investment advice and interact you in implement your instructions and plans.

In the previous Lesson, we laid out the most common options to help you understand the pros and cons of the leading types of investment advisors and how each may fit/not fit into your situation.

Whether you have an advisor now, or are starting the process of interviewing advisors—we suggest starting with the following questions:

Is Your Advisor Working for You? Five Important Questions May Give You the Answer

When determining which type of advisor—and then which specific firm—you may use, the following five questions can be helpful. This is important because the data shows the most investors don't quite know how their advisor makes money. In fact, a 2011 survey by Cerulli Associates and Phoenix Marketing International found that nearly two out of every three investors in the survey were confused about how they were paying their advisors.

This issue made headlines awhile back when a high-ranking Goldman Sachs employee resigned publicly through an Op-Ed piece[9] in the *New York Times*, citing corporate culture as the primary reason for his departure. The employee stated "the interests of the clients continue to be sidelined in the way the firm operates and thinks about making money." If this occurs at Goldman Sachs, whose clients include the most sophisticated financial firms in the world, it can certainly also occur at your chosen investment firm.

The funny part is—this *Times* piece was back in 2012 and—virtually nothing has changed since. That's actually not funny at all. Different groups have tried to appeal to regulators like the SEC and FINRA—even the Department of Labor—to establish a uniform standard requiring all financial advisors to work in the best interests of their clients. To date—not all advisors owe you a fiduciary duty (see Lesson Three for details on different types of advisors).

---

[9] http://www.nytimes.com/2012/03/14/opinion/why-i-am-leaving-goldman-sachs.html.

Here, we will attempt to educate you on five questions you must ask your financial advisor in order to better understand how they make money advising you and how they work for, or potentially against, you. A higher level of transparency will increase your trust level—and trust is the most important component of the advisor-advisee relationship. All the following questions consider transparency and increasing the goal of trust in the relationship.

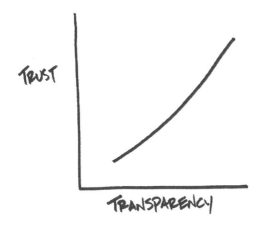

Question #1: Does your advisor owe you a fiduciary duty as a client, or are they held only to a "suitability" standard?

Most investors are not aware of the fact that brokers and investment advisors are held to different standards when it comes to the duty they owe clients. Registered Investment Advisors are held to a "fiduciary standard." This means that we are required to make recommendations that are in the client's best interest. Contrast this duty to the suitability requirement that dictates that brokers are simply required to make recommendations that are suitable based on the facts at the time of the interaction. Recently the Department of Labor has sought to even the playing field by forcing broker-dealers to a fiduciary duty concerning retirement accounts; but the broker-dealer lobby has fought hard against implementation. As of now—only RIAs are held to the higher standard of always looking out for your best interest.

On the surface, this may seem like a subtle difference; however, the end result can have a substantial impact on the client.

Example: Client A contacts his broker and expresses an interest in investing $50,000 in U.S. growth stocks. The broker invests the client assets in Fund XYZ, which charges a sales load of 5.75 percent with operating expenses of 0.68 percent annually. The client will immediately pay a one-time fee of $2875 on the trade on top of the recurring fund–management fee. In this case, the suitability standard has been met. Client B contacts his Registered Investment Advisor with the same request. The investment advisor purchases an ETF with a gross expense ratio of 0.18 percent and pays a commission of $8.95 on the trade. This client pays his RIA a management fee of 1 percent of the assets, which equates to $500 per year on $50,000. The advisor has met the fiduciary standard. In our very realistic example, the front-loaded fees paid by client A are significant enough that it would require a commitment of approximately nine years to this fund family before that commission is equal to the sum of advisory fees paid by client B.

Question #2: Can your advisor provide a detailed explanation of how they are compensated?

Do your advisors receive commissions on any of the investments they will be recommending? Beyond commissions, compensation can come from sales charges on mutual funds or from a higher operating expense on a specific class of funds. A registered investment advisor typically has access to an institutional class of funds which will charge a lower expense than the retail shares commonly offered by brokers.

Private equities, structured notes, hedge funds, and non–traded REITs can offer various fees arrangements that may not be transparent. These investments may have a higher point of entry for an investor under the brokerage model in order to compensate the sales person facilitating the transaction.

A Registered Investment Advisor operating under the fiduciary standard may be able to offer the same investment at a lower cost simply due to the fact that they are not taking a cut before your money goes to work for you.

Example: Client A is approached by his broker to invest in a non-publicly traded real estate investment trust. The client sends in a check for $100,000, and the security is priced at $10 per share, so the client receives 10,000 shares. The broker receives a 7 percent commission from the real estate investment trust sponsor. Client B is approached by his RIA to invest $100,000 in the same privately held REIT. The advisor charges a 1 percent management fee and does not accept compensation from the REIT sponsor. In this scenario, the commission is returned to the RIA client in the form of a reduced purchase price for the shares. Client B receives a discounted price of $9.30 from the sponsor and is able to purchase 10,752 shares of the same REIT with his $100,000 investment. Client A would have to hold the investment for approximately seven years before his 7 percent commission matches the sum of fees paid by client B to his advisor.

Question #3: Does your advisor's firm make money in other ways on your individual investments?

Request clarification on the ways that your advisor's firm may receive financial benefit from the securities you own in your portfolio. As an example, mutual funds commonly offer revenue sharing arrangements with a broker-dealer firm. In this scenario, your advisor at broker-dealer firm XYZ is receiving security analysis provided by its research department, which creates a buy list of securities. Unbeknownst to you, XYZ receives compensation from the fund company offering the recommended products. The result is a higher fee to you, the investor. You will not see these fees appear as a line item on your statement; they will be hidden within the underlying investments. This lack of transparency will not only prevent a client from recognizing the true cost of the relationship; it may also create a bias in the research provided to the client's advisor. This scenario can apply to closed end funds, exchange traded notes, and other securities which will impact the bottom line of the firm, even if your investment representative may not receive additional compensation.

Example: Discount brokerage firm XYZ offers to manage client assets at a reduced cost of 0.80 percent of assets under management for client A. The rep at XYZ purchases $150,000 of retail shares of a bond fund with an operating expense of 0.75 percent. The rep does not receive compensation for choosing this fund; however, his firm (XYZ) receives revenue sharing directly from the fund company. A registered investment advisor for client B charges 1 percent for his services and purchases institutional shares of the same fund with an operating expense of 0.46 percent. RIAs often have access to the lower cost shares offered by certain mutual fund families. In this scenario, the discount brokerage relationship results in a slightly higher cost to client A because of hidden revenue sharing, despite the brokerage charging a lower management fee for their service.

Question #4: Does your advisor utilize proprietary securities?

Proprietary products are not always easily recognizable, as they can be branded under a different name. In-house products are not necessarily poor investments at the moment the recommendation is made to a client. The problem arises when circumstances change and it is no longer in a client's best interest to continue to own the underlying security. Will the in-house research recommend that their team of advisors liquidate the position in each of the firm's client accounts? Consider the impact of mass redemptions in a proprietary security. Who is going to be on the other side of that trade?

Example: XYZ firm runs a highly rated international bond fund with heavy exposure to European bonds. A team of brokers are looking out for their clients and contacts their research team to express concern about the recent drop in price of the investment. The research team of XYZ assures the brokers that they have adequately hedged the portfolio. A month later, concerned about the potential liability of a poorly performing investment, XYZ firm removes the fund from the institutional portfolios they are managing. The large redemptions create a significant drop in the price of the fund. A notification is then sent to the brokers explaining the firm's position after the price drop has occurred. The individual investor has faced substantial losses, while the firm has minimized the damage to their largest institutional clients.

Question #5: Does the advisor's firm engage in investment banking activities?

If the answer is yes, determine how your financial professional (and the firm) is compensated on your purchase of that investment. What is the incentive of the firm to see that the entire offering is filled?

> *Example:* There are countless examples of Initial Public Offerings where individual investors have been sold on tales of tremendous growth opportunities, only to experience disappointing returns and a substantial loss on their investment. The 2012 handling of the high-profile IPO of Facebook resulted in numerous lawsuits and continues to raise questions about the inherent conflicts in the underwriting process.

This is not a complete list of questions to ask your current or prospective advisor, but it is a start. Our hope is that by asking these questions, you will gain a greater understanding of the potential factors that may influence the recommendations of the advisor. If every action made on your behalf is not unequivocally for *your* benefit, it is time to reevaluate the relationship you have with your advisor.

In the next section, we discuss how your investment advisor and wealth management needs may eventually require ancillary coordination with other advisors like accountants, lawyers and other specialists.

Is Your Advisor Part of a Team?

It is extremely important to understand how your advisor works—because you must know their limitations. While you would not expect your CPA or your attorney to give you investment advice—many investors assume their financial or investment advisor is taking into account the tax and legal implications of all their investments.

This is not always the case. Most investment advisors have a core capability—investments. Generally, YOU have to make sure your investment is managing your wealth in a comprehensive manner unless you are working with a wealth management firm that acts as a "quarterback" of your financial life. "Holistic" has become the buzzword *du jour* in the industry. And while many claim to do this—only a few actually deliver.

Having a team working together on your wealth management will answer this question. That said, the right pieces in place is one part of the equation—the other is making certain the pieces work together.

As with any collaborative endeavor, the collection of people into a coordinated team is not enough to ensure success. Every conference call and meeting must have an agenda and someone to manage the meeting to make sure that all-important items are handled within the allotted time. It is common to put one of the advisors in charge of organizing and facilitating information between the other advisors. This is usually a financial planner and not an accountant or attorney—though the "quarterback" could be any one of the advisors on the team. Within the group, you need to identify roles and responsibilities and make one person accountable for the completion of each task.

When considering different options, it is wonderful when there is a unanimous decision on whether to go in a particular direction. However, many decisions will not be unanimous. You need to set the rules (51 percent, 66 percent, 80 percent) on how decisions are to be made within the group and share the rules with the group.

If they know how you are going to make decisions, it will make it easier for them to participate in the group and allow them to continue to participate even when the rest of the group disagrees with a particular decision.

You can't possibly expect to build and protect wealth while holding on to your sanity unless you assemble the right team of advisors. You need to look to specialized financial advisors to provide the greatest financial benefits. You must realize that the process of building and maintaining wealth in today's world brings with it potential challenges from all areas of law, accounting, finance, insurance, and business. When you accept this reality, and embrace the need to leverage the expertise of advisors in all of the areas mentioned above, you will be one step closer to reaching your goals.

As we have discussed in other sections of this book—sometimes the most effective way to accumulate wealth is to just avoid mistakes. The following section addresses common pitfalls associated with leveraging professional advisors. Similar to the medical community—the first adage in wealth management should be 'do no harm.' Review the next section to see if you are subject to any of these common pitfalls.

What to Avoid When Working with Your Advisor (or Your Team of Advisors)

In our many years working with clients, we have seen many make mistakes when selecting and working with their advisors. However, these mistakes can all be avoided. We know this because many of our clients have effectively built their wealth significantly and protected their assets by building the right team of advisors. There are five common pitfalls we have seen when clients choose their advisors:

1. *Choosing Friends or Family as Advisors*

2. *Choosing Only Local Team Members*

3. *"If It Ain't Broke, Don't Fix It"*

4. *Never Getting a Second Opinion*

5. *Hiring Yes Men and Women*

Let's examine each pitfall individually:

Pitfall #1: Choosing Friends or Family as Advisors

One of the biggest mistakes we see is the inclusion of friends and family in the planning team. We can't fault people for thinking that trust is important when choosing people to help manage wealth. Trust is very important. However, unless you are willing to lose the friendship to achieve the financial goals, this should probably be avoided.

It is perfectly acceptable to become friendly with your advisors. This is appropriate because the friendship will have grown out of a business relationship. However, when the relationship instead begins as a friendship, problems may later arise when you disagree on a course of action or when the advisor makes a mistake.

Pitfall #2: Choosing Only Local Team Members

The best available team members need not be the best available advisors in your neighborhood. We have helped clients who built their team with advisors from all four corners of the country. In today's age of technology, information is easily shared through email and online data sharing applications. Don't be afraid to enlist the best advisors you can find—even if they are not in your backyard.

Pitfall #3: "If It Ain't Broke, Don't Fix It"

Having worked with someone for 10 or 20 years is not a reason to continue with the same advisor. If you applied that logic to medicine, patients would still be seeing their pediatricians long after turning 18 years old.

There is a high likelihood that, as you accumulated wealth, your financial needs changed. Though your advisor was there for you when you had simpler needs, you are not required to stay with that advisor when you have outgrown the advisor's, or firm's capabilities and expertise.

The first mistake that many investors make in the financial, legal or tax aspects of their careers is the method they use to initially choose their professional advisors. Whether it was their CPA, investment professional or attorney, many business owners made a poor choice because their method of evaluating the potential advisors was flawed.

When you consider the typical pattern, this is not surprising. Most people chose their advisors when they were starting out and their financial planning and investing needs may not have required much sophistication.

Working long hours, and without the means to evaluate an advisor, young investors typically do what other busy people do and take the path of least resistance. They use the advisor their parents or friends use, or hire a friend or family member.

Though this un-scientific approach is obviously flawed, it serves its purpose when there are bigger challenges at hand. Your life was so hectic that you just needed to "get it done fast." The advisor you chose at that point simply had to be competent and inexpensive—and that was good enough.

What is alarming to us is not this initial choice of advisor, but *the fact that so many investors stay with the same advisors who handled their early planning for the rest of their careers!*

The justification for this is rarely anything concrete or, in our opinion, sufficient to explain why the investor would choose an advisor over his or her own financial security. Answers like "we've been together so long, I'd hate to change now," or "if it ain't broke, don't fix it" are unpersuasive. Further, this begs the question: "How do you know 'it ain't broke' if you don't get a second opinion?"

Most alarming to us—despite the fact that we see it every day –is when an investor stays with an advisor when the investor has clearly outgrown the expertise of the advisor.

> Self-Test: How did you choose the professional advisors you work with today? How many other professionals did you interview prior to choosing one? Have you periodically interviewed others as your needs have changed?

Pitfall #4: Never Getting a Second Opinion

A good way to grade your existing advisors and test the competencies of potential team members is to get a second opinion. Good advisors are busy helping clients like you. They are professionals and will expect to be paid for the analysis. Sure, there are plenty of advisors who will analyze your situation for free, hoping to dazzle you with their recommendations to earn your investment, insurance or legal business. However, the goal of these people is to sell you something.

As mentioned previously, your planning team should consist of talented advisors who want your business—but don't *need* your business. Treat them fairly by paying them for their time and advice. Stepping through this short-term engagement exercise will provide insight into how organized their firm is and how well they communicate.

Of the flaws discussed here, never getting a second opinion is the most damaging. Unfortunately, it is also the most common. It is most damaging because a second opinion is the primary way of identifying planning mistakes or noticeable omissions from your planning.

Just as doctors encourage patients to get a second opinion, good advisors should encourage their clients to do the same. This is the only way for you to adequately judge an advisor's performance. With your entire financial future banking on the success of your professional advisors, it amazes us how few of you have paid another professional to review your existing advisor's work. If your life were in jeopardy, wouldn't you get a second opinion? Isn't your financial life important as well?

> Self-Test: Have you ever paid an outside advisor to review your attorney's work? Your CPA's work? Your investment advisor's work? If not, why not?

Pitfall #5: Hiring *Yes* Men and Women

When we asked numerous successful clients what advice they would give, we received many suggestions. The suggestions included: "find experts," "don't look for 'Yes Men'," and "hire people smarter than you are."

We put them all in the same category because the end result is the same. The wealthy have wealth because they did something very well. The very successful ones realize that they can't be experts at everything. Some rightfully believe that they could focus on finance or law and probably be just as smart as some advisors. They also realize that it would take many years to reach an adequate level of expertise. To leverage their time, they instead choose to hire experts in different disciplines to work for them.

Our most successful clients have told us that they have enough "Yes Men" in their lives. Interestingly, they cherish the moments when advisors stand up to them to challenge their positions or question their decisions. They see this as an opportunity to improve their position. Some even enjoy the challenge.

Warning Signs That You May Be Getting Bad or Outdated Advice

Do any of these "warning signs" that you are ill-advised seem familiar? If so, you are likely suffering from flawed professional advisory relationships:

- *You have had the same advisors for years—and never interviewed other options.*

- *Your advisors don't bring you detailed analyses of your personal situation, complete with helpful suggestions, annually.*

- *You have no idea what the true sub-specialties of your advisors' professions are.*

- *Your present advisors reject ideas you bring to them without providing detailed written explanations of why they don't make sense for you.*

- *Your present advisors have never told you that a certain idea required further research for which they would need to charge you.*

- *You rarely, if ever, have paid for second opinions from other professionals.*

- *You have trusts, partnerships or other legal entities which may not be funded.*

- *There is no coordination among asset protection, tax, investment and insurance advisors on your behalf.*

- *You stay with your present advisor(s) out of lethargy, guilt, or an "if it ain't broke, don't fix it" mentality.*

Only by collaborating with your team of advisors can you properly determine the techniques and tools appropriate for your needs. Together, you can identify your needs, analyze all available options, make a decision and implement the chosen strategies. Once you determine the necessity of professional advice—the next question is how do you properly evaluate the professional you choose.

Understanding How to Track the Performance of Your Wealth Advisor

To determine whether your wealth advisor is performing well, first look to whether they are helping you stay on track to achieve your agreed-upon goals. Further, from a qualitative perspective, note whether you are getting value out of their total wealth management process—including areas such as wealth protection, tax reduction, meeting retirement savings projections, setting and tracking retirement goals, etc.

More quantitatively, some clients tend to look at the investment performance and want to evaluate just this part of their wealth management. In this area, one of the most common mistakes we see is clients comparing their portfolios' returns to the "market"... or the returns of the S&P 500. Let's examine this more closely.

Should You Use the S&P 500 Index as Your Personal Benchmark?

You have certainly heard the argument that most U.S. large company mutual funds do not outperform the S&P 500 on a risk-adjusted basis over an extended period of time. The problem is, as this phrase gets repeated, pieces of the statement are dropped and ultimately investors hear, "*I should put all of my money in the S&P 500*"—or at least track my portfolio against the S&P 500.

Acting on either thought would be a terrible decision for nearly every investor.

Why is putting all your assets in an index a bad idea?

1. An index does not have a time horizon. It will never

retire, face an emergency, find a great deal on a home, lose a job, become disabled, or take a withdrawal for any reason.

2. An index has no emotions. It did not sell after a 20 percent drop in one day on Oct 19, 1987. The index was not concerned about a 55 percent drop from October of 2007 to March 2009. Can you say the same?

3. An index is patient. In the first decade of the 21st century, the S&P 500 provided an annualized total return of effectively 0 percent. By the way, during that 10-year period where your money failed to grow, you also had the joy of experiencing -9.1 percent, -11.9 percent, -22.1 percent, and -37 percent. Would you stay the course?

4. The United States is the largest economy in the world, yet it makes up only 16.1 percent of the global economy as measured by a percentage of world gross domestic product.[10]

If you know for certain that you will never need to take a single dollar from your investments for at least 15 years... and you are comfortable with the potential for a 55 percent loss in your portfolio... then you are in a very small minority of retail investors who could consider placing all investable assets in the S&P 500. This means you have adequate insurance and substantial cash reserves—and, most critically, a mindset to withstand that potential 55 percent drop...or worse.

Most investors are not in such a position—and more than likely, you probably are not either.

Benchmarking
Maybe you need further convincing that the S&P 500 is not the appropriate standard to measure your individual performance (your benchmark). Let's focus on three key reasons why the S&P 500 is an inappropriate benchmark for most investors. The primary

---

[10] see also Lesson 6 for more information on behavioral factors that influence investors to their detriment.

points are:

1. *Investing is emotional* and equities deliver more volatility than you likely realize;

2. *Asset Allocation works*—the largest endowments, institutions, and other ultra high net worth investors choose to diversify because they understand the benefit of maximizing *risk-adjusted* returns;

3. *Time Horizon*—volatility may not negatively impact investors in the accumulation phase of their investment life cycle, if they can avoid succumbing to *fear and greed* (see Lesson Six). Once you approach five to seven years from retirement, however, the narrowing the range of possible outcomes becomes of great importance and can be the difference between success and failure in retirement.

1. Investing is Emotional and You May Not be Equipped to Stomach the Ride

As your assets grow, your appetite for risk will decline. Losing 20 percent of your account value when you have $10,000 in assets, is unsettling. Experiencing a 20 percent decline on a $3 million portfolio, translates to a $600,000 loss (on paper). For many of us, we begin to think "how many years did I have to work and pay taxes, just to save that $600,000 that just evaporated within months?" This begins a cycle of fear which then can lead to selling out when the market is down...even for a mentally-tough investor.

If you still think you can handle such a rapid decline—realize this: you can expect to experience a similar decline every two-to-three years if you invest in an all-equity portfolio!

Double digit intra-year losses in the S&P 500 is the norm, not the exception. Today's investor is more educated and views a ten percent drop in the market as a buying opportunity, however everyone has their breaking point. The difference between successful investors and those who make life-altering mistakes, is understanding *loss threshold*—or knowing your actual tolerance for risk.

Our advice is to design a portfolio with a risk band (and range of risk potential) you can accept. Typically, you need a professional to help stress test your investment portfolio. The majority of investors can accept a 10-15 percent loss. If you are signing up for S&P 500 returns, you are also signing up for potential periods of up to -22 percent (see 2002) or even -37 percent (see 2008) returns. Cumulative returns extending across calendar years deliver more disturbing results.

If you allocated $3,000,000 to an S&P 500 index fund in October 2007, your account would have been valued at $1.35 million in March 2009. Doubling your money every seven years is very appealing, a result the S&P 500 has historically delivered. Unfortunately, these returns are not linear and they do not occur *every* seven years. You cannot predict year-to-year swings as we demonstrate below—you cannot time the market.

Even if you can remove emotion from your equation, there are mathematical reasons to support reducing volatility and avoiding an S&P 500-focused strategy. Why is it important to limit downside? A 50 percent loss requires a 100 percent subsequent return just to breakeven. However, a 10 percent loss only requires an 11 percent return to breakeven!

If you are uncertain about the above, think of our example as compounding in reverse. When working off a smaller base, recovering losses becomes very challenging. Let's look at two hypothetical scenarios:

- Investor A decides to pre-fund his three-year-old daughter's education and invests $100,000 in an S&P 500 index fund late in 2007. Eight months later the account has lost half its value and is worth $50,000. Investor A needs to experience $50,000 of investment gains, on his current $50,000 account. {(Investment gain/account balance)*100=percentage return}

$50,000 Gain Required	*100	= 100% Required Return
$50,000 Current Acct Value		

- Investor B invests $100,000 with his advisor at the same time. The advisor knows Investor B's son is attending college in five years and allocates to a moderately conservative portfolio. Eight months later the account has declined to $90,000. Investor B will need an 11 percent return for his account to return to a $100,000 value.

$10,000 Gain Required	*100	=11.1% Required Return
$90,000 Current Acct Value		

Percentage Loss	Return Required to Breakeven
-10%	11.1%
-20%	25.0%
-25%	33.3%
-50%	100.0%

It may seem obvious—but when you lose small amounts, it's simply easier to make it up. Losing a large chunk of assets is much more difficult to recoup—and generally, when you suddenly need to make up large swaths of ground, it can lead to bad, performance-chasing activity that could put you further in the hole (see the chart in Lesson Two).

2. Asset Allocation Works

There is a good reason pensions, endowments, and the world's most high net worth investors practice the concept of asset allocation. History has proven allocating your assets across multiple fronts; or diversification (see Lesson Two—Diversification: The Golden Rule) is a time-tested method for optimizing your results.

Investors have questioned the benefit of diversification in the midst of many short periods of time throughout the last hundred years. The period from 2012-2016 witnessed one of the more recent exaggerated four-year periods of U.S. equity excessive performance in the history of our markets. Investors should note, despite the period of strength from domestic stocks, emerging market equities were the top performer over a 15-year period.

The chart below (same one we used in Lesson Two—what we learned about diversification 2008) lists the returns of major asset classes by calendar year, sorted vertically by performance. In addition to the five major asset classes, the chart also includes returns for a balanced portfolio and a global stock portfolio. The final column illustrates the average annual return for each asset class over the entire 15-year period.

	2002	2003	2004	2005	2006	2007	2008	2009	2010	2011	2012	2013	2014	2015	2016	15-Year Return
Best	Fixed Income 10.3%	EM Stocks 55.8%	EM Stocks 25.6%	EM Stocks 34.0%	EM Stocks 32.1%	EM Stocks 39.4%	Fixed Income 5.2%	EM Stocks 78.5%	US Small Stocks 26.9%	Fixed Income 7.8%	EM Stocks 18.2%	US Small Stocks 38.8%	US Large Stocks 13.7%	US Large Stocks 1.4%	US Small Stocks 21.3%	EM Stocks 9.5%
	EM Stocks -6.2%	US Small Stocks 47.3%	Dev Intl Stocks 20.2%	Dev Intl Stocks 13.5%	Dev Intl Stocks 26.3%	Global Stocks 11.7%	Balanced Portfolio -22.8%	Global Stocks 34.6%	EM Stocks 18.9%	US Large Stocks 2.1%	Dev Intl Stocks 17.3%	US Large Stocks 32.4%	Balanced Portfolio 6.0%	Fixed Income 0.5%	US Large Stocks 12.0%	US Small Stocks 8.5%
	Balanced Portfolio -9.4%	Dev Intl Stocks 38.6%	US Small Stocks 18.3%	Global Stocks 10.8%	Global Stocks 21.0%	Dev Intl Stocks 11.2%	US Small Stocks -33.8%	Dev Intl Stocks 31.8%	US Large Stocks 15.1%	Balanced Portfolio 1.9%	US Small Stocks 16.3%	Global Stocks 22.8%	Fixed Income 6.0%	Dev Intl Stocks -0.8%	EM Stocks 11.2%	US Large Stocks 6.7%
	Dev Intl Stocks -15.9%	Global Stocks 34.0%	Global Stocks 15.2%	Balanced Portfolio 5.2%	US Small Stocks 18.4%	Fixed Income 7.0%	US Large Stocks -37.0%	US Small Stocks 27.2%	Global Stocks 12.7%	US Small Stocks -4.2%	Global Stocks 16.1%	Dev Intl Stocks 22.8%	US Small Stocks 4.9%	Balanced Portfolio -1.5%	Global Stocks 7.9%	Global Stocks 5.9%
	Global Stocks -19.3%	US Large Stocks 28.7%	US Large Stocks 10.9%	US Small Stocks 4.9%	Balanced Portfolio 15.8%	Balanced Portfolio 6.8%	Global Stocks -42.2%	US Large Stocks 26.5%	Balanced Portfolio 12.6%	Global Stocks -7.3%	US Large Stocks 16.0%	Balanced Portfolio 12.1%	Global Stocks 4.2%	Global Stocks -2.4%	Balanced Portfolio 7.8%	Balanced Portfolio 5.7%
	US Small Stocks -20.5%	Balanced Portfolio 21.0%	Balanced Portfolio 9.9%	US Large Stocks 4.6%	Balanced Portfolio 12.5%	US Large Stocks 5.5%	Dev Intl Stocks -43.4%	Balanced Portfolio 19.9%	Dev Intl Stocks 7.8%	Dev Intl Stocks -12.1%	Balanced Portfolio 12.1%	Fixed Income -2.0%	EM Stocks -2.2%	US Small Stocks -4.4%	Fixed Income 2.6%	Dev Intl Stocks 5.3%
Worst	US Large Stocks -22.1%	Fixed Income 4.1%	Fixed Income 4.3%	Fixed Income 2.4%	Fixed Income 4.3%	US Small Stocks -1.6%	EM Stocks -53.3%	Fixed Income 5.9%	Fixed Income 6.5%	EM Stocks -18.4%	Fixed Income 4.2%	EM Stocks -2.6%	Dev Intl Stocks -4.9%	EM Stocks -14.9%	Dev Intl Stocks 1.0%	Fixed Income 4.6%

See appendix for magnified chart

Note the randomness—if you are looking for a pattern, you will be disappointed. Even if you could detect a pattern—it would be worthless because the past performance would not work as an indicator or predictor of future results.

What if we take a global approach and look back to 1970? The chart below illustrates a global equity portfolio has not only outperformed the S&P 500, the globally diversified portfolio has managed to deliver superior results with *less* risk (standard deviation is a measure of risk, the higher the number the more volatile a portfolio). Starting at $100,000—invested in 1970 through 2015; the Global Equity portfolio outperformed a 100 percent (S&P 500) U.S. stocks portfolio by $28,428,637.

	Annualized Return 1/1/1970 to 12/31/2016	Standard Deviation 1/1/1970 to 12/31/2016	Starting Value	Ending Value
Global Equity Portfolio	10.9%	14.8%	$1,000,000	$128,915,089
100% U.S. Stocks (S&P 500)	10.3%	15.4%	$1,000,000	$100,486,452

See appendix for magnified chart

The world's most affluent investors have decided against allocating their entire net worth to a single asset class *i.e.* putting all their eggs in one basket. Why? Experienced high net worth investors understand assets move in and out of favor.

The following chart shows a breakdown of high net worth investors'[11] financial assets (by region). This graphic demonstrates how high net worth investors invest broadly to mitigate risk. The diverse allocation keeps these investors from trying to predict and choose the top performer every year. Spreading the investments out also keeps them from jumping from one category to another— thus generating capital gains which bring a healthy tax liability. Affluent individuals in all regions allocate their funds to real estate, fixed income, alternative investments, and cash equivalents. The percentage they dedicate to any particular type of investment may differ—but note how in each region they generally avoid high concentrations in any one specific type.

---

[11] A high net worth investor is commonly defined as an investor with
$1 million in liquid financial assets.

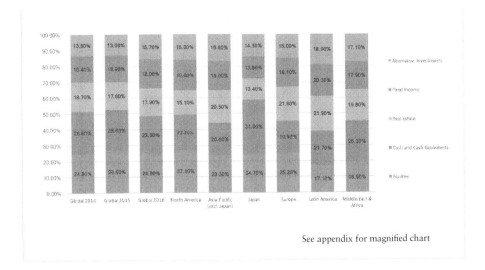

See appendix for magnified chart

The sophisticated investor understands the best way to ensure consistent growth net of taxes and inflation, is to not become dependent on one asset or one index. Experienced high net worth investors do not benchmark their cash, municipal bonds, or their art against the S&P 500. They understand the risk metrics are not the same. Consequently, these same investors are not consumed with the results of a single equity index against their entire net worth.

3. Time Horizon: Understanding all Returns are not Created Equal
The sequence of your returns may also be a crucial investing success factor depending on where you are in your life—especially when you *are* retired and as you *approach* retirement.

If you have a lump sum investment, and do not add to or withdraw from the account, the order of your returns will not make much of a difference in the final outcome. The emotional roller coaster you experience will be different based on the sequence of returns—the positive returns can come early in the period or late. Your balance at the end of the period of time will be the same. However, the real world does not work this way. Investors are adding to accounts monthly or annually via company sponsored retirement accounts or regular deposits into a brokerage account.

The impact the sequence of returns has on a successful retirement once an investor begins taking distributions must be considered. As an investor approaches retirement, risk management becomes the most critical component of investment planning. Narrowing the range of possible outcomes is the difference between a successful retirement allowing you to pass a legacy onto your children, and running out of money.

Hypothetical example

Year	PORTFOLIO A		PORTFOLIO B	
	Return	Balance	Return	Balance
0		$100,000		$100,000
1	-15%	$80,750	22%	$115,900
2	-4%	$72,720	8%	$119,772
3	-10%	$60,948	30%	$149,204
4	8%	$60,424	7%	$154,298
5	12%	$62,075	18%	$176,171
6	10%	$62,782	9%	$186,577
7	-7%	$53,737	28%	$232,418
8	4%	$50,687	14%	$259,257
9	-12%	$40,204	-9%	$231,374
10	13%	$39,781	16%	$262,594
11	7%	$37,216	-6%	$242,138
12	-10%	$28,994	17%	$277,452
13	19%	$28,553	19%	$324,217
14	17%	$27,557	-10%	$287,296
15	-6%	$21,204	7%	$302,056
16	16%	$18,796	13%	$335,674
17	-9%	$12,555	-12%	$290,993
18	14%	$8,612	4%	$297,433
19	28%	$4,624	-7%	$271,962
20	9%	$0	10%	$293,658
21	18%	$0	12%	$323,297
22	7%	$0	8%	$343,761
23	30%	$0	-10%	$304,885
24	8%	$0	-4%	$287,890
25	22%	$0	-15%	$240,456
Arithmetic Mean	6.8%		6.8%	
Standard Deviation	12.8%		12.8%	
Compound Growth Rate	6%		6%	

See appendix for magnified chart

NOTE: Sequence of returns risk revolves around the timing or sequence of a series of adverse investment returns. In this example, two portfolios, A and B, each begin with $100,000. Each aims to withdraw $5,000 per year. Each experiences exactly the same returns over a 25-year period—only in inverse order—or "sequence." Portfolio A has the bad luck of having a sequence of negative returns in its early years and is completely depleted by year 20. Portfolio B, in stark contrast, scores a few positive returns in its early years and ends up two decades later with more than double the assets with which it began.

Readers are likely to be shocked by the results of the illustration above. The hypothetical example demonstrates two investors taking 5 percent of the initial principal. Portfolios A and B have the exact same return over a 25-year period with identical risk. Portfolio A ran out of money. Portfolio B experienced a 140 percent increase in value at the conclusion of the 25-year period. Your initial feeling may be complete despair, recognizing you have no ability to influence market returns in retirement. Neither investors or advisors can control the timing of stock returns, however they can control risk. By managing risk, you can manage the range of possible outcomes, ultimately increasing your odds of success. The portfolio illustrated in the chart above was too aggressive given the income need of the investor.

What are the Odds of a Negative Equity Return?

The retirement income chart might give the impression retirement planning is nearly impossible due to the threat of negative returns. You obviously need to minimize negative investment performance when possible during your asset accumulation phase and as you approach the distribution phase of your investment life cycle. Understanding the odds of an adverse investment outcome, can serve as a valuable tool when designing an investment portfolio. If the S&P 500 is used as the benchmark to determine the odds of down market, you will find negative returns occur approximately once every four years. Extending your time horizon, means the likelihood of a negative return declines. Rolling ten-year periods where the S&P 500 experiences negative returns are rare, historically occurring slightly more than 5 percent of the time. Five-year rolling periods of negative returns are more than twice as likely to occur. The probability of negative returns may be low, however you are not going to care about statistics and probabilities if you experience a steep decline in principal the year you wish to retire (or in the years immediately preceding retirement).

TIME FRAME	POSITIVE	NEGATIVE
Daily	54%	46%
Quarterly	68%	32%
One Year	74%	26%
Five Years	86%	14%
10 Years	94%	6%
20 Years	100%	0%

A comprehensive wealth management plan will help you strategically plan to weather negative market performance years—regardless of when they happen. We will touch on the importance of comprehensive wealth management throughout this book—for now, simply note the importance in regards to benchmarking via the S&P.

I Still Believe My Advisor Should Beat the S&P 500... Isn't that what I'm Paying for?

You must understand there is no free lunch when it comes to risk and reward. Outperforming any benchmark over an extended period of time means you are assuming a similar, or higher, level of risk as the actual benchmark. The best money managers in the world may demonstrate an ability to beat their specifically-chosen benchmark by a marginal amount, *however they are not doing so by taking less risk*. If the goal is to outperform a benchmark, you must expect the manager or advisor to take 90 to 115 percent of the risk of the respective benchmark which they are measured against.

Example: Assume you have set the standard for your advisor to beat the S&P 500 index. After a few decades of hard work, you have accumulated $3 million in investable assets and are two years from retirement. The S&P experiences a year similar to 2002 and declines 23 percent. Your advisor outperforms the S&P 500 by a whopping 5 percent. The accounts you have spent years accumulating are down $540,000 and your $3 million is now less than $2.5 million. Your advisor delivered exactly what was asked and then some. Are you satisfied with the result?

The purpose of the example above, is to demonstrate if the S&P 500 declined 23 percent and your investments lose 18 percent, there is a high probability you will not be complimenting your advisor. Why not? Your advisor has only exceeded the expectations you instructed and achieved the stated goal.

Let's look at another example illustrating why setting a goal of outperforming the S&P 500 is a flawed strategy.

> An investor has told his advisor he is expected to outperform the S&P 500 index. The advisor recognizes that if he designs a portfolio with more risk than his benchmark, he will outperform the benchmark more often than not. An aggressive portfolio is created, intending to take 115 percent of the risk of the index. In the interest of maintaining simplicity, let's assume the portfolio performs exactly as intended without tracking error. Returns are 15 percent higher versus the benchmark in positive years... but also 15 percent lower in down years.
>
> The investor's $1,000,000 portfolio as illustrated below, has outperformed in three of five years: a 60 percent success rate. Not only has the portfolio delivered a higher rate of success, it has a higher average annual rate of return over the five-year period. The advisor has accomplished the stated goal; therefore, his client should be satisfied.
>
> Of course, one fairly significant detail has been overlooked: The strategy generating a lower average return and more consistent results, completed the five-year period with a larger ending balance.

Year	S&P Return	Beginning Value	Year End Value		Year	Portfolio Return	Beginning Value	Year End Value
1	14%	$1,000,000.00	$1,140,000.00		1	16.10%	$1,000,000.00	$1,161,000.00
2	19%	$1,140,000.00	$1,356,600.00		2	21.85%	$1,161,000.00	$1,414,678.50
3	-14%	$1,356,600.00	$1,166,676.00		3	-16.10%	$1,414,678.50	$1,186,915.26
4	-26%	$1,166,676.00	$863,340.24		4	-29.90%	$1,186,915.26	$832,027.60
5	20%	$863,340.24	$1,036,008.29		5	23.00%	$832,027.60	$1,023,393.65

What is the lesson to take away from the example? Beating (or trying to beat) the S&P 500 may not be as appealing as you have been led to believe. Just to try to beat it requires taking an equivalent level of risk (or more) to outperform the S&P 500 on a consistent basis. This is not suitable for the vast majority of investors. If you are in the minority and happen to have an extremely high risk tolerance, you should still note: outperforming the index at a successful rate may not result in a larger ending lump sum.

Investors should be less concerned with the results of an index, and more concerned with achieving long term *consistent* growth. Professionals in the financial industry have preached the need for investors to seek long term consistent growth, without obsessing over the performance of an index. So why do investors remain skeptical of what they are hear from advisors?

First, because the industry has done a poor job illustrating the need to limit volatility versus chasing performance. Second, probably more important in a theoretical setting, many people will say that they accept the risk required to achieve better-than-S&P performance. However, most people are truly not willing to accept the risk that comes with chasing high performance—when the true risk is adequately explained and illustrated. Even fewer people can actually stick with such a high-risk strategy when they experience worse-than-index performance in down years (like years 3 and 4 above).

This is due to the theory of loss aversion. Human beings have a natural tendency to prefer avoiding losses over acquiring equivalent gains. Numerous studies have suggested the psychological impact of a loss is *twice* as powerful relative to a comparable gain. Amos Tversky and Daniel Kahneman performed extensive research on this topic.[12]

Investors tend to underestimate the psychological[13] impact of loss, and they also severely underestimate the risk associated with investing in the S&P 500. The job of an advisor is to help investors develop a better understanding of these topics, and in turn develop

---

[12] Tversky and Kahneman wrote extensively on the irrational way many individuals, and groups of individuals make decisions. The Michael Lewis book, *The Undoing Project*, is a great summary of their work. Also consider reviewing Daniel Kahneman's *Thinking Fast and Slow*.

[13] See also Lesson Six—information on cognitive bias and other reasons investors often make bad investing decisions.

a better understanding of themselves.

Human beings are (typically) not wired to handle the volatility associated with a single index—especially the S&P 500. You are hiring your advisor to perform planning and prevent you from making life altering mistakes—not just to beat an index.

My advisor should convince me to take less risk, however isn't their job to identify when the largest risks are occurring and get me out of the market at that time?

An advisor is not going to jump in and out of the market every time a sell-off occurs. If you have found an advisor that consistently does this effectively, congratulations! You can stop reading. The next call will be from your CPA to let you know the brilliant trading from your advisor has generated short-term capital gains on all your positions. These securities were held for less than twelve months and taxed as ordinary income. If in the top bracket, you just lost 43.4 percent of your gains. You may also be subject to state income tax on your successful trades. Consequently, certain individuals may pay more than 50 percent on short-term capital gains. Not only are you asking your advisor to choose the perfect time to get out of the market and to choose the perfect time to reinvest, you are also asking them to overcome the 15 to 50 percent tax liability you may be subject to from short-term trading (assuming a portion of your investments are in a non-retirement account)! That said, nobody can consistently time the market—anyone claiming this ability is ignorant or a fraud.

Your personal goal should not be to beat the S&P 500 or some other random index—it should be to accumulate enough wealth to retire on your terms when you are ready.

Success during your accumulation phase will be impacted by your ability to accept the short-term losses associated with investing.

As you get closer to your envisioned retirement, risk management becomes the most critical component of investing and wealth management. Managing risk could be the difference between a successful retirement on your terms—and having to work longer or running out of money. Success or failure will not be determined by one's skill "getting in and out" of the market, which is exactly why neither an advisor nor an investor should be engaged in market timing.

How Do I Measure Success: What Should Be *My* Benchmark?

This is a great question and frankly, the answer depends on you. It would be great if there was an easy, *one-size-fits-all* solution, but the fact is, each investor's circumstances and risk tolerance is different. What works for you—will not work for your neighbor.

A 65-year-old who intends to retire in two years and immediately take income from investments, should have a very different benchmark than a 30-year-old with 100 percent of their investable assets in a 401(k).

Where Should *You* Start?

First, you must determine when you will need access to the funds you are investing. The longer the time horizon, the greater probability you will end up with a larger pool of assets by increasing equity exposure.

Next, really understand your risk tolerance. The biggest mistake an investor can make is selling assets in their portfolio immediately after a decline. Not only may you incur taxes on top of the transaction costs, but when will you decide it is "safe" to re-invest? In Lesson Six, we will show you the monumental opportunity cost you face if you miss even a few days out of the market each decade. If you re-invest even a little too late, you could lose the equivalent of years of upside.

Remember markets are forward-looking. If you make a decision based on bad news, this information has already been priced into the financial markets. If you need to have a conservative allocation to avoid making this mistake—it is a perfectly acceptable position provided you have enough stock exposure to outpace inflation.

Finally, work to develop your investment philosophy and stay committed to that approach. Another critical mistake[14] investors repeatedly make is chasing performance. A frustrating component

---

[14] See also Lesson Six for more details regarding the most common mistakes investors make.

of diversification and asset allocation is that you will always lag the hottest investment...but you will also never finish below the worst performing asset class. Again, see our chart on Winning/ Losing Asset classes back in Lesson Two.

One of our core beliefs is that an investor should minimize expenses whenever possible, and reduce volatility by owning securities across a variety of asset classes. An investor's goal should not be to outperform the top asset class every year. The objective should be to achieve an average targeted return which will allow him/her to reach their goals.

You advisor's job is to generate the optimal return given the appropriate level of risk you are willing to accept. The latter part of the prior sentence is often forgotten; an advisor's role is not to simply seek maximum return. Work with your advisor to find a blended benchmark which is a reasonable point of reference for your portfolio.

Morningstar is one firm that creates a series of blended benchmarks—ones that clients and advisors often utilize to evaluate investments. A blended benchmark is a hypothetical portfolio of indices, including exposure to U.S. stocks, foreign stocks, bonds, and cash equivalents. Utilizing an appropriate benchmark will create reasonable expectations and allow for a healthy dialogue between client and advisor.

Conclusion

It is important to understand how your advisor works for you.

Many investors hire financial advisors simply for peace of mind. Having a professional looking out for you—someone who is studying financial markets and economic data on a daily basis— allows a large segment of investors to sleep at night. It is one less thing you must worry about—or at least one less thing you have to worry about as often.

Understanding how your advisor or their firm makes money and to whom they owe their duty (you or their firm) is a paramount first step in finding the right professional to guide you. Asking the right questions of your advisor to get accurate answers is crucial. Then, coordinating the investment advisor you choose with your comprehensive wealth management, and evaluating their work for you are the key ongoing challenges.

We hope that the last two Lessons were helpful in beginning this process.

Wealth Management Strategy and Planning

"Successful investing takes time, discipline and patience. No matter how great the talent or effort—some things just take time—you can't produce a baby in one month by getting nine women pregnant."

—Warren Buffett, Chairman and CEO Berkshire Hathaway

 In Part I, we covered common investment terminology and reviewed market history for background and perspective. Part II covered the importance of working with professional, trusted advisors to increase your performance to build more wealth. Part III covers managing your wealth and investing in a clear, strategic manner to help avoid succumbing to the ebbs and flows of market volatility.

We also cover the necessity of planning beyond your investments and how investing fits into comprehensive wealth management, culminating in a holistic plan.

Manage Your Wealth Strategically

*"Most investors want to do today
what they should have done yesterday."*

—Larry Summers, former U.S. Treasury Secretary,
President of Harvard University, economist and professor

We all live in a *now* society. Everything seems to be available on-demand—but you generally cannot achieve wealth overnight. For most people, it takes time and patience.

 In the previous Lessons, we reviewed the historical performance of the markets to show their volatility. Unpredictability and volatility are scary. It is human nature to gravitate towards things we can control—even if it's just the illusion of control. Having a sense that we are in control is comforting and calming.

In our opinion, the simple approaches are best—because a simplified strategy can weather more storms and generally they do not require that every detail break a certain (positive) way.

Our Investment Approach

We use asset allocation to mitigate market risk. We also closely study valuations to find, and take advantage of, the occasional *Fat Pitch*. Good wealth managers do this by:

1. Establishing a strategic or "neutral" allocation for each portfolio type.

2. Shifting asset allocation away from neutral only when there are "fat pitch" opportunities:

    - When one asset class is extremely undervalued relative to competing asset classes

- When we can make high-confidence assessments of the impact of cyclical factors that might enhance shorter-term opportunities

3. Using risk analysis to test the portfolio's exposure to various types of downside risks.

4. Making decisions based on at least a three-year time horizon.

5. Analyzing and choosing index funds, and, in some cases, actively managed mutual funds, to implement the chosen asset allocations.

What is a Neutral Allocation?

A *neutral* allocation reflects a sensible, static, *strategic* asset allocation for a hypothetical long-term investor (depending on their time horizon, risk tolerance, *etc.*). It is the starting point for our *tactical* asset allocation process.

What is the Purpose of Neutral Allocation?

1. The neutral allocation is a portfolio's asset allocation that we will fall back to when our conviction level about any specific asset class is not high enough to justify changing the asset allocation mix. It gives us a baseline long-term allocation that is based on thorough research and historical experience.

2. The neutral allocation gives us a constant frame of reference against which to measure each decision. For example, if we like REITs and want to add them to a client's now-neutral allocation, we must decide what they will replace in the portfolio and how far from neutral we are willing to move. This will be a function of our confidence and the impact on the portfolio's risk and return potential. The permanent frame of reference imposed by the neutral allocation assures that we will consistently apply our methodology. It is this discipline

that is so valuable. Consistent application of a discipline is critically important to investment success.

How to Arrive at the Neutral Allocations for Each Portfolio Type?

First we identify risk tolerances, defined as a maximum loss over various periods of time. Then we look at many different combinations of asset classes over many historical periods. Through numerous iterations of adjusting the asset class mix, and looking at the results over various historical periods (over 80 years) that reflect differing circumstances, we arrive at neutral allocations that:

1. Have very high statistical probabilities of staying within the stated risk tolerance for each model. (Though the probabilities are in the high 90 percent range, they are not 100 percent—there is no guarantee that risk levels will not be exceeded going forward.)

2. Are diversified enough to provide some smoothing of performance.

3. Have delivered, over the average 10-year period, a higher return than a simple S&P 500/bond mix with slightly less variability (in the case of equity portfolios, a higher return with less variation than the S&P 500.)

4. Make sense given what we know about the investment climate today.

Shifting from Neutral— "Swinging at Fat Pitches"

Our active asset allocation process (decisions to diverge from neutral), involves making asset class moves only when we have a very high degree of confidence that the moves will pay off in the short or medium-term (i.e. 3-4 years). Using a baseball analogy, we only want to swing at "fat pitches" (i.e. pitches that are over the center of the plate that we are likely to hit).

It is important to understand there is a difference between timing the market, and taking advantage of opportunities over the course of a market cycle. If you pay attention, you can occasionally spot the proverbial *fat pitch*.

What is a *Fat Pitch*?

Financial markets are quite efficient—most assets are priced fairly (based on all publicly available information) most of the time. This means that most of the time it is difficult to "outsmart" the market. However, the market does, occasionally, offer investors exceptional opportunities. Capturing a portion of the return from these opportunities, and locking them in for a full market cycle, can result in market-beating performance over a cycle.

Warren Buffett puts it well when he refers to the manic/depressive nature of *Mr. Market*—despite all the information that investors have at their fingertips, irrational *greed* and *fear* occasionally drive the market for financial assets. It isn't the norm, but it happens.

While recognition of these opportunities might not make you wealthy (a good plan will do that), identifying fat pitches can add to your bottom line. Here are a few hypothetical scenarios:

- If the current environment has created a steep yield curve (a term defining a large spread between short-term and long-term interest rates) are you able to identify the industries positioned to outperform?

- The world's largest consumer economy is experiencing little to no wage growth. Do you understand the relationship between wages and inflation, and if so how do you profit from that information?

Our discipline allows us to shift our portfolios only when we have very strong indications that the odds are heavily in our favor because the market is not pricing rationally—a generally rare occurrence for asset classes. This may mean little activity in some years. Importantly, by only swinging at fat pitches (and patiently waiting for them), we minimize mistakes by not making shifts when the financial markets are not giving us a compelling opportunity.

Why Swing ONLY at Fat Pitches?

Swinging only at fat pitches is not the only way to invest successfully. However, too many investment professionals and retail investors believe that investment success requires lots of activity. This is wrong.

Our methodology is to *swing only* when we have very strong indications that the odds are heavily in our favor because the market is not pricing rationally. This is a rare occurrence for asset classes—meaning little activity in some years. If you think about it in baseball terms—we take what the pitchers give; we take our walks—take easy swings and hit singles—but if everything lines up perfectly; a hitters count, a weak pitcher, men on base—we swing a little harder.

Importantly, by only swinging at fat pitches (and patiently waiting for them), we minimize mistakes (make fewer outs) by not making shifts when there simply are no fat pitches to swing at—not swinging when Mr. Market is neither manic nor depressive.

So, only when the markets are clearly acting irrationally regarding a specific opportunity will we take action on that specific opportunity. When they are rational, we won't try to make something out of nothing—even if it would provide for the appearance of doing more for a client. Sometimes the best action is inaction. The market rewards patience—we can get further along not making outs—rather than swinging hard and striking out.

It only takes a few fat pitches over a market cycle to make a difference. But it takes discipline and focus to have the patience to wait for the opportunity, and intestinal fortitude to act when the markets are irrational. Successfully executing a fat-pitch strategy will add value to long-term performance relative to the neutral allocation (a successful long-term investment strategy in its own right).

How to Find a Fat Pitch?

First, we believe it is critical to apply a consistent approach to identifying fat pitches. This is part of our discipline. Our research suggests two important factors:

1. An extreme undervaluation (or overvaluation) relative to alternative asset classes.

    In measuring this undervaluation, we first compare equity assets (foreign stock opportunities, small companies, REITs) to the S&P 500. In comparing the portfolio's total equity exposure, we then compare valuations to investment grade bond yields.

2. The stage of the "risk cycle" can enhance or detract from the valuation argument.

Research strongly suggests that extreme undervaluation in a particular asset class indicates a material period of outperformance is in store in the not too distant future. Many factors may cause the asset class to appear moderately undervalued when it is not. The fat pitches we will swing at will probably be the result of a bear market or a severe correction. This is when the depressive side of Mr. Market shows his face, often in the form of panic selling, causing extreme undervaluation.

Further, if we believe we are beginning a new market cycle (or very close to it) anticipating an economic recovery, this enhances the valuation-driven fat pitch. Not only would this produce great valuations, but also an expected end to the fear-driven psychology that created the undervaluation. On the other hand, if we are late in the cycle but not at the end of it, investors may continue to be cautious, avoiding the riskier assets that usually get beaten up in bear markets (economically sensitive assets and less liquid assets such as small-caps and REITs). This makes the fat pitch slightly less fat, but may not invalidate it totally. Most of the time, severe undervaluation coincides with a cyclical bear market when both factors are working together.

It is helpful to think of the market cycle as a risk cycle. As markets move past their early and mid-cycle strength, investors tend to temper their enthusiasm for riskier equity assets. Though the enthusiasm for equities in general remains high, even growing— often leading investors to avoid less liquid or potentially more volatile asset classes. In an economic downturn, after markets have taken the cyclical hit, investors begin to anticipate a recovery, and there is less of an inclination to avoid these riskier assets because of the expectation that the next downturn is a long way off. Thus, a new risk cycle begins.

One problem is that investors may not know for sure whether a bear market marks the end of an economic cycle until after a rebound has occurred. Our discipline, which focuses on extreme undervaluation, will typically prompt us to take a slightly over-weighted position in an asset class before this occurs. We would then increase exposure as we become more confident that a cycle is ending—even if valuations are not quite as good (though they would still be excellent relatively). If we don't get to this point, we would not add to the position and would unwind it at a lower relative valuation than if we knew we were early in the cycle.

How Can We Be Confident There Will Be Fat Pitches in the Future?

Our high confidence that there will be fat pitches rests on the observation that fear and greed have always moved markets. When fear turns into panic, investors truncate their time horizons. They don't care about three years, or perhaps even six months. This reaction can create tremendous values for those with a discipline that allows them to maintain reasonable time horizons. A strong discipline, consistently applied, can give us the strength to act when others allow fear to cloud their decision-making. It will be especially important to avoid swinging at bad pitches as we wait for opportunities.

Isn't this Akin to Market Timing?

No. Valuation doesn't tell us anything about timing. We expect this discipline to lead us to overweight early (before a bottom) and get us back to or below our neutral allocation before a top. But we have no expectations for stop-on-a-dime market timing. In fact, our discipline is more likely to lead us to reduce exposure far before a market peak than close to a peak.

When There is a Fat Pitch, How Much Will We Buy or Sell?

This will depend on the portfolio. The more aggressive the portfolio, the wider our discretion to overweight or underweight each asset class. We're also biased toward capital preservation in our more conservative portfolios and maximizing return in our more aggressive portfolios. The allocations will also depend on whether we believe we are early in cycle, in addition to an extreme valuation opportunity.

How Do We Take Advantage of Fat Pitches?

In certain equity asset classes, we will, at times, use index funds to overweight asset classes (relative to the neutral allocation). Our reasoning is that our research will focus on the opportunity with respect to the asset class, so we want to ensure that we capture the future performance of that asset class. Over short and intermediate periods, there is risk that a manager may be out of sync with the asset class—especially managers who run concentrated portfolios (in general, we do have a bias towards these types of managers.) Using an index fund eliminates this risk. When we use actively managed funds to implement an overweighting, they will be well-diversified funds that we expect will closely track the index. We will also consider tax efficiency for taxable portfolios.

Though index funds have the reputation of being tax efficient, this depends on the index. As an example, small-cap index funds have often not been very tax efficient.

When Will We Use Active Managers?

For some asset classes, there are no index funds. For others, active managers have been so dominant that it is harder to justify using the index. There are other asset classes for which we'll have to consider specific factors, such as the Japanese weighting in some international index funds (though it is much smaller than it used to be).

In most cases, we will use active managers for long-term positions that form the permanent core of our neutral allocations. We do extensive due diligence on managers, and only use those managers in whom we have a very high level of confidence in their ability to continue to outperform a benchmark.

Conclusion

We cannot control the markets. Even if we have a complete understanding of all the components of our plan, we cannot predict how they will act under pressure in volatile markets. No matter how well you know the rules, once the game starts you can't predict what your opponent is going to do. But you can study. Football coaches look for tendencies in their opponents to gain an advantage—using their opponent's predictability against them. Chess players do the same. In baseball, pitchers and hitters study each other to try and predict how each other may act under differing sets of circumstances like whether they are ahead or behind in the count. You can never know for sure what your opponent will do, but if you know enough about them—you can accurately predict some of their moves.

It's tougher to accurately predict the where and when in market movement. We all know the market will go up, go down and move along sideways—we don't always know when or why. However, if we know and embrace the volatility—we can use it to our advantage.

There are various strategies you can employ to attempt to gain greater yield and boost your investment performance. Yet the best strategy is still a strong, disciplined strategy designed to meet your long-term goals.

Having the right wealth management plan in place will get you through the highs and lows that history has shown will continue to come. Having a flexible plan will help you make the right adjustments at the right time—rather than adjusting on the fly, based on the latest news cycle.

It is simple—but not easy. You must fight against your own impulses. The next Lesson details how we often sabotage our own wealth management by acting in completely normal ways.

Adopt a Winning Mindset and Avoid the Most Common Mistakes

"The investor's chief problem—and even his worst enemy— is likely to be himself."

—Benjamin Graham, Professor,
Economist and the father of value investing

"The four most dangerous words in investing are: 'this time it's different.'"

—Sir John Templeton, investor, philanthropist and
Manager of the Templeton Growth Fund

You may have heard the axiom in sports "the best offense is a good defense." It is a clichéd line—but clichéd for a reason; it's often true. Sometimes the best way to make progress is to avoid making mistakes. Employing a wealth management strategy built around avoiding the biggest mistakes would outperform many of the most aggressive strategies in the long run.

In our practice, we have found the majority of mistakes investors make are self-inflicted. In prior Lessons, we discussed the importance of patience.

One of the most valuable aspects to working with an advisor is they will help you sort through all the noise and avoid the most common and costly mistakes.

Why Market Timing Fails: The Data on Individual Investor Behavior

Individual investors get crushed in the long run when they try to time the market—even in times when the investment itself has done well. As we described in the introduction, performance of an *investor* does not equate to the performance of the *investment*. This is simply due to the basic human emotions *greed* and *fear*. Several studies (summarized below) show how and why this happens.

Human nature works against you in investing. Retail investors tend to buy into the market near the top of a cycle—when their *greed* kicks in ("the market has been going up—I want in on this!"); only to sell at close to the market's low when *fear* rules the day ("the market is getting killed—I better get out before it's too late!"). This is an obvious recipe for disaster.

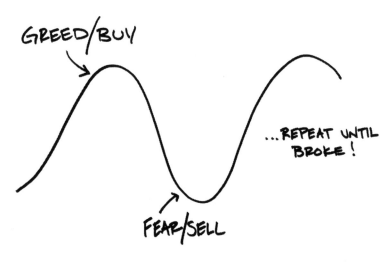

GREED/BUY

...REPEAT UNTIL BROKE!

FEAR/SELL

© 2013 Behavior Gap

Dalbar Study

The first study we will take a quick look at is the Quantitative Analysis of Investor Behavior study; generally known as the Dalbar Study.[15] Dalbar, Inc. is a well-known firm that evaluates, audits and rates business practices of investment companies, registered investment advisors, insurance carriers and other financial professionals.

Their study on investor behavior has been published every year since 1991. The main objective as stated by the researchers themselves is "to improve the performance of independent investors and investment advisors by managing behaviors that cause investors to act imprudently."[16] The study attempts to provide some guidance on how and where investors behavior can be improved.

Per the 2015 Dalbar study, the average equity mutual fund investor underperformed the S&P 500 index by a wide margin of 8.19 percent in 2014 (13.69 percent vs. 5.50 percent).

In other words; if the average equity investor had taken a passive approach with their mutual funds—they would not have underperformed so dramatically. Note; we explained in Lesson Four

---

[15] Dalbar's 21st *Annual Quantitative Analysis of Investor Behavior*; 2015 Advisor Edition; www.dalbar.com

[16] *Id.*

why benchmarking against the S&P 500 Index is not generally the best way to benchmark performance. For now, we will explore why it is so difficult for individual investors to manage their own behavior when it comes to *passive* investing and how this negatively affects their wealth.

To further illustrate that this wide margin was no 'one-off' outlier, we need to look at the long-term statistics. The 20-year annualized S&P 500 return was 9.85 percent versus a mere 5.19 percent for the average equity mutual fund investor (a 4.66 percent gap). A $100,000 investment over 10 years equates to a difference of $57,691.14. Applying the same scenario to a $1,000,000 portfolio means a difference of nearly $577,000.

The Dalbar's data suggests that behavioral factors (outlined below) cause most investors' greed/fear reactions to kick in. This leads to a *cycle of loss* that starts when the investor abandons their plan (if they have one) and gets out of the market at the worst possible time—followed by a period of remorse as the market recovers. What do they do to next? They re-enter when the news media starts pontificating on how great market is doing.

The Dalbar study further discusses three causes of investor shortfall. Many simply 1) do not have available capital to invest; or 2) they have capital, but they need it for other purposes. That said, even if you have the available funds for investing, the study found that; 3) psychological factors will still likely be the biggest barrier to your investment performance.

The study unequivocally states, "investment results are more dependent on investor behavior than on fund performance."[17]

We will cover the psychological factors in detail below, but first we will summarize a second study showing the cost of attempted market-timing.

Morningstar Research

 Morningstar provides investment research to professional investment advisors and the general public. They also research investor behavior. Morningstar's research continually shows the devastating price investors pay in

---

[17] *Id.*

attempting to time the market. Morningstar monitored mutual fund investors' cash flow for ten years. They used investor returns to determine how the average investor fared during the decade. The total return for the average investor in all funds between 2000–2009 was 1.68 percent, compared with 3.18 percent for the average fund itself.

Morningstar determined that most investors read too much into *recent* performance (bias)—letting fear and greed influence their decisions, making bad situations worse.

Investors lost over 47 percent of the fund performance due to their market timing decisions. In other words, an investor who did not try to time the market, but stayed in for the highs and lows, performed nearly 94 percent better than those who tried to time it.

A review of actual historical data further shows individual investors tend to not only sell assets at the worst time, when the market sell-off has reached or is near the lows, they also *fail to re-enter the market* when it does finally reach a "bottom."

No one can tell you the precise moment the market has reached its low or its peak—it is only in hindsight that you can recognize that data. No one on this planet knows the exact timing of either of those extremes. Market timing isn't hard—it is impossible.

Morningstar also looked at the related issue of the importance for the individual investor to stay invested, as opposed to timing exits and entrances based on market movements—in another study. They stated:

> "The image illustrates the value of a $100,000 investment in the stock market during the period 2007–2016, which included the global financial crisis and the recovery that followed. The value of the investment dropped to $54,381 by February 2009 (the trough date), following a severe market decline. If an investor remained invested in the stock market over the next 82 months, however, the ending value of the investment would be $195,719. If the same investor exited the market at the bottom to invest in cash for a year and then reinvest in the market, the ending value of the investment would be $127,517. An all-cash investment at the bottom of the market would have yielded only $54,580. The continuous stock-market investment recovered its initial value over the next three years, and provided a higher end-

ing value than the other two strategies. While all recoveries may not yield the same results, investors are well advised to stick with a long-term approach to investing."

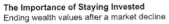

The Importance of Staying Invested
Ending wealth values after a market decline

See appendix for magnified chart

Not only does jumping in and out of the market cause lower performance; but investors also succumb to increased trading fees and face possibly significant tax consequences when they decide to sell an entire portfolio moving the assets to all cash. Thus, the true "net" numbers for investors may be significantly worse than the numbers Morningstar references above.

Only Missing a Few Days Can Have a HUGE Impact

If you accept that market timing does not work and that it will cost you significantly over the long run, the question then becomes: How much?

The following image illustrates the risks of attempting to time the stock market by showing the effects of missing the best month of annual returns between 1970 - 2016.

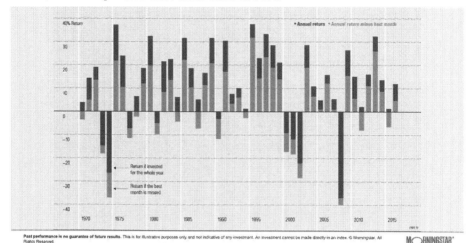

See appendix for magnified chart

Missing the one best month during a year drastically reduces returns. During years when returns were already negative, the effect of missing the best month only exaggerated the loss for the year. In seven of the 47 years shown (1970, 1978, 1984, 1987, 1994, 2011, and 2015), otherwise positive returns would have been dragged into negative territory by missing the best month.

Let's look at what happens if you miss only a few days in the market. It might surprise you to learn how much an investor can lose by missing even a few days of the market over a long period.

Below is a graphical depiction from Morningstar displaying the impact of missing the best trading days in the S&P 500 over a 20-year time frame spanning from 1994-2013:

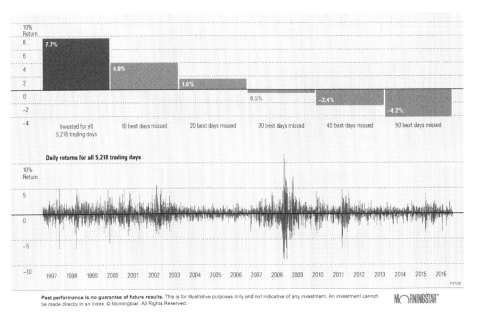

See appendix for magnified chart

The data above shows that by missing only 50 of the best 5,040 trading days during this time period, you would have seen your compound annualized return go from +9.2 percent to a -2.8 percent.

Missing only 10 of the best days–or one trading day every two years–would have cut your annualized return from 9.2 percent to 6.6 percent–a reduction of over 28 percent of your returns during this time period. For many retail investors, this is astounding. This is obviously a drastic performance deviation despite being out of the stock market for a mere 0.2 percent of the time.

Although short-term successful market timing may improve portfolio performance, it is very difficult to time the market consistently. In addition, unsuccessful market timing can lead to a significant opportunity loss.

Richard Bernstein Advisors LLC embarked on a similar study to the Morningstar and Dalbar studies. The graphic below provides a depiction of the actual returns of various asset classes vs. an average investor over a 20-year period:

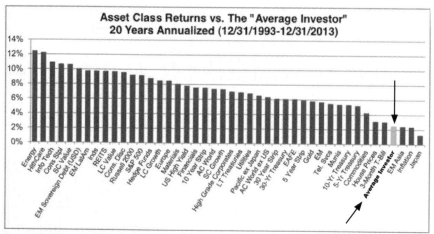

**Asset Class Returns vs. The "Average Investor"
20 Years Annualized (12/31/1993-12/31/2013)**

Source: Richard Bernstein Advisors LLC., Bloomberg, MSCI, Standard & Poor's, Russell, HFRI, BofA Merrill Lynch, Dalbar, FHFA,
FRB, FTSE. Total Returns in USD.
Average Investor is represented by Dalbar's average asset allocation investor return, which utilizes the net of aggregate mutual
fund sales, redemptions and exchanges each month as a measure of investor behavior.
For Index descriptors, see "Index Descriptions" at end of document.

See appendix for magnified chart

The above chart compares the 20-year investment performance of the average investor—to the performance of twenty asset classes and sub-asset classes. Investors with a savvy wealth management plan will likely have some of these classes. The chart demonstrates the poor performance of the typical investor by showing they have underperformed every category except Asian emerging market and Japanese equities—coming in 41st of 43 studied categories.

Typical investors even underperformed cash (shown above as 3-month T-bills). They could have simply improved their performance by buying and holding any asset class (other than Asian emerging market or Japanese equities). The likely cause of their underperformance is the continual attempted timing decisions—investors consistently bought assets that were overvalued and sold assets that were undervalued. Buying high and selling low—the *cycle of loss*.

So, what should *you* do to avoid this cycle? Put all your available capital in a long term diversified portfolio and leave it alone until you need it? That is one approach—an approach that will beat the *cycle of loss*. However, the *set-it-and-forget-it* approach has its own shortcomings.

First, circumstances in your life will change—and these changes will require revisiting your wealth management plan. But notably, most investors simply cannot stick to a set-it-and-forget it plan. See information below on where investors go wrong to see why it is so difficult to stay the course without help.

Where Do Investors Go Wrong?

As shown above, the spread between market returns and investor returns is dramatic—and the costs of getting such timing wrong are huge. Why do we do this to ourselves?

The first and most easily recognizable reason is emotion. It is important to note that emotional decision-making is the number one enemy of investors, and is exactly where most go wrong.

Logic tells you when an item is inexpensive then you have reached the optimal time to buy. You or your spouse has likely spent hours in search of value trying to minimize the price you pay for goods or services. Investors should apply the same logic to buying stocks. However, data shows that most people do the opposite. Money is emotional, and losing it (even if only on paper) impacts most investors in a manner that prevents them from applying reason.

Financial markets are forward looking, anticipating events 12-18 months in the future. If you are acting based on the most recent news, you are actually acting on information that has already been priced into the market. The financial media (more on this later) does not perform any favors to the investing public. The 24-hour news cycle often provides the impression you need to sell your holdings at the first hint of negative news—that you must act, and act now. Action in haste in investing is almost always a bad idea.

Crisis and panic keeps viewers tuned in. Sound advice is unlikely to top the Nielsen ratings. An advisor may not be able to identify the bottom of the market, however if you have reached a point where you can no longer handle the losses, there is a good chance you have found the floor for equities. One poor decision driven by emotion can set you back years.

We will revisit emotion and how it impacts your investment

decisions. In the meantime, all the following information is provided to demonstrate why *investments* do fine—but *investors* flounder. Remember this illustration from the introduction?

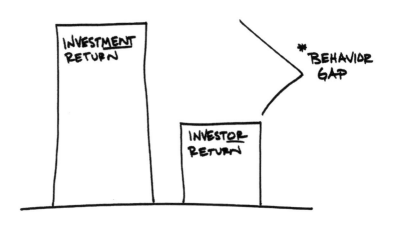

Keep this *behavior gap* in mind as we address the most common issues that often cloud our judgment every day—in investing and other areas.

Herd Mentality

Individual investors are not the only ones guilty of group thinking, but it is an especially common occurrence on Wall Street. Human nature suggests we like to have our opinions accepted and validated. Holding a viewpoint similar to the majority may be a recipe for a successful political career, however it is not always an advisable investment strategy.

One of the most egregious examples of the herd mentality was the dot com bubble in the early 2000s. Companies with negative earnings were experiencing 300 percent stock returns in quick six-month time periods. Everyone was convinced the internet was going to revolutionize the world. Investors could not fathom being left behind, tossing aside any consideration of fundamentals.

It turns out investors were partially correct, the internet did change the way we conduct business, gather information and even how we live our lives. But what did that mean for tech stocks? The tech weighted NASDAQ took 15 years to reach the levels it achieved in 2000.

The dot com bubble was an extreme example of a mentality among investors that continues to exist today. A contrarian indicator followed by many analysts, is the trend of mutual fund inflows from individual investors. These contrarians avoid or underweight the sectors of the market experiencing the largest flows from retail investors.

Poor decision making from individual investors has historically occurred with such frequency, that there is actually a dumb money index followed by several analysts. Please don't be upset with us; we did not create the name! We could provide an overwhelming amount of data and statistics to support the herd mentality viewpoint. The reality is our industry is often guilty of data overload, adding an unnecessary layer of complexity to matters.

Consider this simple example: XYZ stock is up 150 percent in two years. Everyone in the financial media loves the stock and raves about the company. You read your favorite financial publication and see XYZ is among the most heavily owned securities by hedge funds. Finally, your mother who has never shown a hint of interest in investing is asking you if she should buy XYZ stock. Ask yourself this: Who is left to buy the stock?

The two prior examples are the most common reasons for underperformance of the individual investor. However, the following also work against individual investors' portfolios driving underperformance.

Cognitive Bias: Reasons the SEC Believes Individual Investors Make Bad Investing Decisions

We spoke above about the most common, broad reasons why individual investors often underperform. The following information is even more detailed information about how our emotions work against us when it comes to money and investing.

There is a large barrier standing in the way of performance and it is you.

Not just you—every individual investor.

Why are individuals so hard pressed to outperform the market? Let's take a deeper dive into the relatively novel concept of **behavioral finance** as well as exploring the main reasons behind the inability for many individual investors to get out of their own way.

Psychological pressures surround all of us throughout various aspects of our lives and are often heightened or increased during periods of extreme uncertainty, causing us to exhibit extreme and irrational behavior.

For proof of this we will explore multiple aspects of investor 'misbehavior' to determine the overall impact on portfolio returns.

Why Do We Act This Way? Eleven Common Individual Investor Mistakes

In 2010, the Securities and Exchange Commission Office of Investor Education and Advocacy requested that The United States Library of Congress Federal Research Division prepare a report on the behavioral traits of U.S. retail investors.[18] The report identifies nine common investing mistakes that affect investment performance. These traits are common behavioral characteristics that work against your investment returns, usually because you are too emotionally involved in the decision-making process.

- **Active Trading** —is the practice of engaging in regular, ongoing buying and selling of investments while monitoring the pricing in hopes of timing the activity in order to take advantage of market conditions. Active traders underperform the market. For the average retail investor, constant activity and speculation is detrimental to their long-term performance. A good advisor should assist in you in creating a

---

[18] The full report available as of March 30, 2017 at url: https://www.sec.gov/investor/locinvestorbehaviorreport.pdf.

long-term strategic plan that does not involve churning or activity for the sake of activity.

- **Market Timing**—how difficult is it for the "average investor" to actually identify and correctly time market fluctuations (both in the short and long term)? The answer tends to be not all that well. When you look at actual historical data, individual investors tend to not only sell assets at the worst time (when the market sell-off has reached or is near the lows), they also fail to re-enter the market when it does finally reach a "bottom" (after all no one actually tells you in that moment that the market has reached the lows or the highs—it is only in hindsight that we can digest that information).

- These investors attempt to sidestep the natural ebbs and flows of the global stock markets. What they fail to often realize is that you have to make the correct "call" not once but twice—an investor that may exit the stock market early, thus avoiding a portion of the downturn in the market, will also need to re-enter the market once that trough has been reached (I am going out on a limb here and stating that no one on this planet knows the exact timing of either of those extremes and, if someone actually had that precursory knowledge, they would be on an island somewhere not telling anyone of their fortune-telling ways!)

- **Disposition Effect**— is the tendency of retail investors to hold losing investments too long and subsequently sell winning investments too soon. Most people are risk averse—even more so when handling their own investments. Loss-averse investors tend to sell high performing investments in hopes of offsetting losses from losing investments.

- **Paying More Attention to the Past Returns of Mutual Funds than to Fees**— Many retail investors pay too much credence to the past performance of mutual funds while virtually ignoring the funds transactional costs, expense ratios and fees. These types of fees can have a significant drag on the performance of your portfolio if they are not accounted for. Your advisor should account for fees in any analysis of your holdings. Remember, it is not only the performance of the fund that matters, but ultimately the value you get out of it.

- **Familiarity Bias**—is the tendency of many investors to gravitate towards investment opportunities that are familiar to them. This bias leads to investing in glamor stocks or glamor companies, investing too heavily in a local stock, or employees investing too heavily in their employer's stock. A good advisor will work to ensure you are aware of being overly concentrated in certain areas and they will seek to keep your portfolio properly diversified in order to limit exposure.

- **Mania/Panic**—Mania is the sudden increase in value of a "hot" investment, wherein the masses rush to get in on the action. Panic is the inverse, where everyone tries to get off of a sinking ship. What is the next "bubble"? When will there be another "crash"? With the advent of the 24-hour financial news channels, social media and other concentrations of constant financial information, investors are now more than ever, susceptible to mania and panic. All the noise leads to the next common factor...

- **Noise Trading**—which often takes place when the investor decides to take action without engaging in fundamental analysis. When an investor follows too closely the daily headlines, false signals and short-term volatility, their portfolios suffer. Long-term plans require picking investments via economic, financial and other qualitative and quantitative analysis. Advisors take emotion out of the equation and seek to build your plan to weather manias and panics and keep you from following the herd fueled by the noise of the day's leading story.

- **Momentum Investing**—is the practice of buying securities with recent high returns and selling securities with low recent returns assuming the past trends and performance will continue. Chasing momentum leads to speculative bubbles with the masses inflating prices. Similar to manias and panics, retail investors are often the last ones to know either way, causing them to often jump on a security experiencing momentum at the wrong time, usually buying high and selling low—with obvious detrimental effects on their portfolio.

- **Under-Diversification**—happens when the investor becomes too heavily concentrated in a specific type of investment. This increases their exposure by having too many eggs in one basket. It goes without saying that any long-term investment plan requires diversification. However, retail investors generally need the assistance of an advisor to diversify correctly. Otherwise, they may be susceptible to the next common error.

- **Naïve Diversification**—is the practice of an investor deciding to diversify between a number of investments in equal proportions rather than strategic proportions. Proper diversification in the investment arena is not simply putting X asset classes in X equal percentages. Rather, a proper allocation strategy should weight your differing investments in a manner in line with your personal risk tolerance in order to build value over the long-term. Keep in mind the asset class *Winners and Losers* chart from Lesson Four that demonstrates how difficult diversification is.

- **Recency Bias**—humans seem to be hardwired to continue to do what has worked for them in the past; the old saying goes, "If it ain't broke, don't fix it." Certainly you could argue this makes sense in many aspects of life, one of them however is not necessarily investing.

Avoiding FRAUD—Five Tips from the SEC

 As you have just reviewed, many behavioral and psychological factors blind us to bad decisions when it comes to investing. Unfortunately, they often blind us to outright fraud. Why do we fall for these seemingly easy-to-avoid financial traps?? Because we want the lies to be true. We want to believe in quick and easy investments with no risk and high returns.

Not every opportunity is a good opportunity—especially in wealth management. Some opportunities will simply not fit into your plan based on your timeline or your risk tolerance. Other "opportunities" should be avoided for more insidious reasons—fraud.

With the advent and popularity of the internet and social media, there has been a considerable trend in fraudulent investment opportunities offered via direct-to-consumer/investor channels.

In 2014, the SEC issued an Investor Alert to "help investors be better aware of fraudulent investment schemes that may involve social media." With investors increasingly exploring new avenues for information—many are turning to Facebook, Twitter, LinkedIn, Youtube and other social networks to research opportunities, securities, background information on advisors, and for general guidance on investing. Social media seems to move in real time—thus many monitor their feeds for up-to-date financial news, or to chat and trade information with others in online forums. Social media is a key tool for many investors—including professionals.

Social media can provide many benefits, but it also presents increased opportunities for fraud.

Nothing beats common sense. If you take one single lesson away from this section: note—if it sounds too good to be true—it probably is. Be vigilant and educate yourself before considering any online investment or opportunity promoted on social media. Here are five tips from the SEC Investor Alert on avoiding investment fraud online:

1. Avoid Unsolicited Offers

Criminals promoting fraudulent investments look for victims on social media sites, chat rooms, and other popular forums. If you receive a notification, a direct message, an email, or any unsolicited message regarding any type of investment opportunity, you should more often than not, run the other way. At a minimum, exercise extreme caution. Many scams use spam to reach potential victims because it is cheap, easy and hits the largest potential audience. Spammers can send literally millions of personalized messages to people and it is far less expensive than traditional methods like cold calling or hard mail. If you receive an unsolicited message online containing a *can't miss* investment with low risk, and high returns, your best move is to pass and report it to the SEC Complaint Center.

2. Look out for Common *Red Flags*

These tips essentially apply to all investment opportunities—if you receive a recommendation for an investment; whether it comes from an advisor, a friend or from social media, the following *red flags* should cause you to proceed with caution prior to acting:

- **It sounds too good to be true**—any opportunity that sounds/feels too good to be true probably is. Be extremely wary of hyperbole—any claims that an investment will make "INCREDIBLE GAINS" or is a "BREAKOUT STOCK PICK" or has "HUGE UPSIDE AND ALMOST NO RISK!" Hyperbolic claims are hallmarks of extreme risk or outright fraud—unfortunately they work, because we want them to be true.

- **The promise of *guaranteed* returns** is a sure sign that you are being duped. Every investment entails some level of risk. Read that again—every investment includes risk, including total loss of principal. The risk is reflected in the rate of return you should expect to receive; meaning

if your investment is 100 percent safe, you'll
most likely get a low return. Hucksters try to
convince investors that high returns are *guaranteed* or that the investment can't miss. Investments can and do miss and no legitimate investment can guarantee you great returns without
incurring risk.

- **High pressure sales tactics** to buy now—before
  you miss out! Never be pressured or rushed into
  an investment before you have a chance to think
  about, investigate and research the opportunity.
  Be skeptical of all investments—this will force
  you to explore all opportunities and potential
  avoid confirmation biases and falling prey to
  believing things you want to believe. Any opportunity pitched as *once-in-a-lifetime* is probably
  fraudulent. If the promoter claims the recommendation is based on inside or confidential information—it may be fraudulent and/or illegal.

3. Affinity Fraud

The SEC defines *affinity fraud* as investment scams that
prey upon members of identifiable groups, such as reli-
gious or ethnic communities, the elderly, or professional
groups. Never invest based solely on the recommendation of a friend/family member or member of an organization or group to which you belong. Any pitch made
through an online group of which you are a member,
or from a chat room, may be an affinity fraud. Even if
the offer seems legitimate and you personally know the
person making the investment offer—check out everything, no matter how trustworthy the person seems who
brings the investment opportunity to your attention.
Because the person telling you about the investment
may have been fooled into believing that the investment
is legitimate when it is not.

4. Privacy and Security Settings

Anyone who uses social media as a tool for investing

should be mindful of the various features on these websites designed to protect their privacy. If you do not guard your personal information, it may become available not only for your friends, but for anyone with access to the sites you visit. This tip is really two-fold. First, protect yourself when using your personal wifi and public wifi networks. Signing in to banking, broker-age or other accounts on public networks could expose all your information to other hacking and snooping on the same network. Second, be mindful of what you post on social media sites—sharing personal informa-tion makes it much easier for identity thieves and other hackers to pose as you online.

5. Question, Vet and Check Out Everything

Be skeptical. Be skeptical of every opportunity. Vet and research every offer before making a decision to commit any funds. Investigate the investment thoroughly and check the truth of every statement you are told about the investment. You can check out many legitimate investments using the SEC's online resources. You can check out registered brokers at FINRA's BrokerCheck website and registered investment advisors at the SEC's Investment Advisor Public Disclosure website.[19]

Common Investment Scams Using Social Media and the Internet

Things move fast online. Fraudsters are constantly trying to stay ahead of protections by changing the way they approach victims. That said, there are a number of common scams that you should be aware of and on the lookout for when using social media:

- **"Pump-and-Dumps" and Market Manipulations:** these are schemes involving touting of a company's

---

[19] The SEC has a great resource with questions to consider asking about prod-ucts and questions for prospective advisors at: https://investor.gov/system/files/publications/documents/english/sec-questions-investors-should-ask.pdf.

stock (typically small, so-called "microcap" companies) through false and misleading statements to the marketplace. The false claims generally appear on social media. Pump-and-dump schemes often occur online where it is common to see messages urging to buy a stock quickly or to sell before the price goes down. Promoters claim to have inside information about an impending development; or claim to use an algorithm or other nonsensical tool that analyzes economic and stock market data and picks guaranteed winners. Usually it is the promoters who gain by selling their shares after the stock price is pumped up by the buying frenzy they falsely create. Once the investment hits a high enough mark, the fraudsters dump their shares and stop hyping the stock—then the price falls and you lose your money.

- **Online Investment Newsletters, and Spam Blasts—** There are many legitimate online resources and newsletters that contain useful information about investing. Unfortunately, others are tools for fraud. Worse yet—they can all look the same—making it difficult to determine the good from the bad and ugly. Fraudulent promoters can claim to offer independent, unbiased recommendations in newsletters even though they stand to profit from convincing their readers and subscribers to buy or sell certain securities (usually penny stocks). These resources and newsletters may be advertised and promoted on legitimate websites, including on the online financial pages of mainstream news organizations, but this does not mean that they are not fraudulent. Companies can pay online resources and newsletters to tout or recommend their stocks. Touting itself is not illegal—provided the source discloses that they are paid promotors; including who paid them, how much they're getting paid, and the form of the payment (cash or stock). Fraudsters often lie about the payments they receive and their track records in recommending stocks.[20]

- **Internet-Based Offerings**—the SEC defines offering fraud as an offering involving a security/investment offered to the public, where the terms of the offer are materially misrepresented. These offerings usually make misrepresentations about returns and risks. Online offerings may not be fraudulent *per se*, but may otherwise fail to comply with the applicable registration requirements and federal securities laws. Federal securities laws generally require the registration of solicitations or offerings, with some exemption. To be safe, always check to see if a securities offering you are considering is registered with the SEC or a state, or is otherwise exempt from registration, before investing any funds.

Social media permits contact with many different people at a relatively low cost. It is easy to create a slick, seemingly legitimate site with email and direct message capabilities. It is that appearance and feeling of legitimacy that gives criminals a better chance to convince you to send them your money. They play on our fear and greed impulses—we want high reward and low risk, easy and cheap investments opportunities—but these do not exist. Trust your instincts. If it sounds too good to be true…it is.

Finally, it can be virtually impossible to track down online fraudsters that use social media. The anonymity makes it difficult to recoup funds and for fraudsters to be held accountable. Use caution on social media in general, but especially when considering an investment.[21]

---

[20] You can find additional tips for checking newsletters and other resources from the SEC at: https://www.sec.gov/investor/pubs/cyber-fraud/newsletter.htm.

[21] For more information, check out:https://investor.gov/additional-resources/news-alerts/alerts-bulletins/updated-investor-alert-social-media-investing, and/or https://investor.gov/protect-your-investments/fraud/types-fraud

Conclusion

The above factors demonstrate why individual investors do poorly on their own. An experienced advisor should be aware of the common mistakes made by individual investors. A good advisor understands the feelings his or her clients are experiencing, but they are usually able to detach themselves from responding emotionally and make educated decisions.

We will spend the final Lesson discussing the importance of creating and maintaining a holistic wealth management plan.

Build and Maintain a Path— Planning for Success

"By failing to prepare—you are preparing to fail."

—Benjamin Franklin

A 2015 survey by the American Psychological Association[22] found that money is the leading cause of stress among Americans—especially for parents, younger adults ages 18 to 49 years old and, not surprisingly, those living in lower-income households. For the majority of Americans (64 percent), the survey found money is a "somewhat" or "very significant" source of stress.

A recent Stress in America™ survey showed that stress about money and finances is prevalent nationwide, even as aspects of the U.S. economy have improved. In fact, regardless of the economic climate, money has consistently topped Americans' list of stressors since the first Stress in America survey in 2007.

- Seventy-two percent of adults report feeling stressed about money at least some of the time and 22 percent say that they experience extreme stress about money (a rating of 8, 9 or 10 on a 10-point scale about their stress about money during the past month).

- Twenty-six percent of adults report feeling stressed about money most or all of the time.

- Significant sources of money-related stress reported by Americans include paying for unexpected expenses, paying for essentials and saving for retirement.

---

[22] *Stress in America: Paying With Our Health* (February 4, 2015) American Psychological Association; accessed online on March 1, 2017 via url: https://www.apa.org/news/press/releases/stress/2014/stress-report.pdf.

- Thirty-two percent of adults say that their finances or lack of money prevent them from living a healthy lifestyle.

- Twelve percent of Americans have said they skipped going to the doctor in the past year when they needed health care because of financial concerns.

 Why are we all so stressed out about money? Why do we continue to stress about money—even when by most logical standards, we have enough to provide the most basic, yet essential, needs for our families? The reason we all stress about money is because we are all afraid that we will run out. No matter how much you have—it is a basic fear that you may lose it. Losing it could mean having to live a standard below what you are accustomed to; or it could mean being destitute. There is a lot of room in between.

There is no silver bullet guarantee that you will never lose everything—but you can mitigate the risk considerably by simply engaging in wealth management planning. Prior Lessons helped you recognize the pitfalls of most investors going alone and the importance of working with an advisor—but where do you start?

Your Wealth Management

Strong wealth management is an ongoing process. It is a dynamic, flexible blueprint that outlines the steps you will take to reach your goals. Your plan should help you make sensible decisions about your money that can help you achieve your goals in life. It should not be a *set-it-and-forget-it* static plan and it's not just about buying financial products. It might involve putting appropriate wills in place to protect your family, thinking about how your family will manage without your income should you fall ill or die prematurely, planning for education costs, protecting your assets from lawsuits and creditors, or, most likely, it involves thinking about all of these things together.

When investors have a plan, they are more likely to apply a holistic approach to their financial lives. Not having a plan is what causes investors to get off track and ultimately leads to destructive behavior. A lack of planning opens the door to excessive spending, performance chasing, and compulsive trading driven by fear and greed.

Our vision of the best possible wealth management is a plan that provides you evolving, well-coordinated wealth management that fits *your* needs. The plan should have an advocate/leader or *Financial Quarterback*—the person who will field your first call when you have a question concerning any financial matter.

The Planning Process

The Standards of Professional Conduct (Standards) define financial planning as "the process of determining whether and how an individual can meet life goals through the proper management of financial resources. Financial planning integrates the financial planning process with the financial planning subject areas."

They discuss six steps to the financial planning process:

1. Establishing and defining the client-planner relationship
2. Gathering client data including goals
3. Analyzing and evaluating the client's current financial status
4. Developing and presenting recommendations and/or alternatives
5. Implementing the recommendations
6. Monitoring the recommendations

Do You Have a Plan? Do You Understand Your Plan? Is Your Plan Up-to-Date?

We are consistently surprised by how many people we meet who cannot answer the above questions. More concerning, however, is how many people we talk to who answer *no* to the above questions.

We all have excuses for putting off financial planning:

- It's time consuming.

- It's hard to face past financial mistakes.

- It's hard to think about the future when I barely have time to plan for today.

While partially valid, the reasons above should not be an excuse for not planning for your future. If you do not have a plan—there is good news: it is never too late to start.

We will discuss further below. If you do have a plan—it is paramount that you understand the plan.

- What is the timing of your plan?

- What are the goals of your plan?

- How often are you revisiting the plan?

Having a plan is not enough—you must stick to it. You must update the plan. A wealth management plan is not a *set-it-and-forget* model. In this Lesson, we try to dispel a few myths about planning and try to provide some quick guidelines and hopefully some inspiration for starting or revisiting your plan.

Your Plan Evolves with You

It is important to understand the unique challenges and planning that must be in place during the different phases of your life.

Accumulation Phase: A period of time when clients are in the early stages of building up their assets. This period begins when you enter the workforce and begin setting aside funds for later in your life, and ends when you actually retire.

Distribution Phase: When you retire, and start collecting money from the retirement income sources that you set up during the accumulation phase of your life, you can be said to have entered the distribution phase.

During your *accumulation phase*, you are earlier in your career and family life. You have many responsibilities to both, often running from meeting to meeting and then soccer field to baseball game. Because you are younger, there is a long-time horizon for investments.

During this phase, you are increasing your income, but your spending needs are many times at their highest. Although you are finally earning "real money" and have the capacity to begin saving, your net worth is likely quite small. It may even be negative if you have significant debt from student loans, home mortgage, or car loan. During this phase, your priorities may be liquidity for emergency funds, buying your initial or larger home, starting a family, and saving for your children's education.

While you may not have significant savings, starting to invest as early as possible is best. In considering suitable investments, you should focus on relatively high-risk, high-return, capital-gain oriented assets.

Your *distribution phase* is the time in your life when you start collecting on the various investments and retirement savings accounts you've set up throughout the rest of your life. You are no longer *building* wealth, but *using* your wealth you've accumulated to fund your retirement.

Start Early

It seems obvious, but the sooner you start—the better off you will be. Due to the long-time horizon, you have a greater probability of riding out the ups and downs of high-volatility (i.e. high-risk) investments that offer greater potential returns. You really can't afford to wait, because the longer you wait, the more you'll need to save. The sooner you start, the more difference it can make! Let's compare two hypothetical people.

Example: Maria and Steve

Maria started saving at age 25. She put away $5,000 (approximately $416 per month) each year for 10 years. Then she *stopped* contributing, but allowed her savings to stay invested until she retired at age 67.

Steve started saving later, at age 35, (the same time

Maria stopped), he put away $5,000 each year for 32 years. He retired at 67 as well.

If we assume both earned a hypothetical 7 percent annual rate of return on their money every year—this is what it looks like when they hit retirement:

Steve accumulated $571,761
Maria accumulated $624,653

Let's take a deeper look at the numbers. Maria contributed $110,000 less yet came out $52,892 ahead. Why? Because her money had a longer time to grow—the power of compound interest.

Keep in mind while Steve was saving, Maria stopped! If she had kept saving until she turned 67, she'd have over $1,196,414.

How do these numbers affect your retirement?

What if you're older or closer to retirement? If you consider that the average retirement lasts 20 years, *you still have time* to invest your money and make it work for you, even when you're retired. So, you're never too old, or too young to start investing—and to take advantage of the compounding potential. And there's never a better time than *now*!

Now that you know that you have to save, consider our discussion on where to find the money you need to save for retirement.

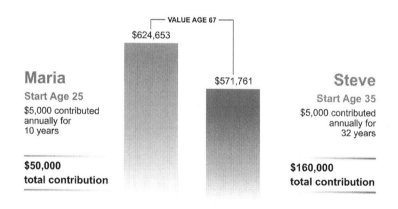

VALUE AGE 67

$624,653

Maria
Start Age 25
$5,000 contributed annually for 10 years

$50,000
total contribution

$571,761

Steve
Start Age 35
$5,000 contributed annually for 32 years

$160,000
total contribution

This hypothetical example is based on monthly contributions of $416.66 for Steve and Maria, made at the beginning of the month to a tax-deferred workplace savings plan and a 7% annual rate of return compounded monthly. Your own plan account may earn more or less than this example, and income taxes will be due when you withdraw from your account. Investing in this manner does not ensure a profit or guarantee against loss in declining markets. 582769.2.1

Distribution or spending phase commences at retirement as employment or business income ceases or slows. Your debt should be gone or significantly reduced, your children grown and no longer needing support and your required expenses should not be extensive.

The burden for covering living expenses in retirement is increasingly shifting to individuals. Generally, if you don't save enough for retirement, you have three options:

1. retire later,

2. retire in a much different lifestyle than you had planned, or

3. don't retire at all

Look at the following chart, which is based on an analysis by the Social Security Administration, and how "guaranteed income" sources have shifted over time, as well as the National Association of Variable Annuities' (NAVA) research on potential new products for retirement income.

In 1974, 56 percent of retirement income came from federal sources (such as Social Security) and private pension plans. By 2010, that number dropped to just 36 percent of retirement income, making the average retiree responsible for 64 percent of their income in retirement. And, without a pension plan source, the number jumps to an alarming 81 percent. Fast-forward to 2030, and we can see that only 24 percent of guaranteed income is anticipated to come from Social Security and pension plans. That means the average retiree will have to rely on their personal savings as well as the possibility of working in retirement.

Today's retirement landscape

Where the money is really coming from

Sources of Retirement Income

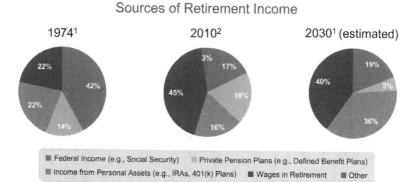

1974[1]   2010[2]   2030[1] (estimated)

■ Federal Income (e.g., Social Security)   ■ Private Pension Plans (e.g., Defined Benefit Plans)
■ Income from Personal Assets (e.g., IRAs, 401(k) Plans)   ■ Wages in Retirement   ■ Other

[1] Source: Research on Potential New Products for Retirement Income, FCNBD, May 2006; National Association for Variable Annuities (NAVA), "2005 Retirement Fears," March 28, 2005. Survey of 1,001 nationally representative Americans age 18+, conducted by Kelton Research, January 2005.

[2] Source: Social Security Administration, Income of the Aged Chartbook, 2010. SSA Publication No. 13-11727Released: March 2012. Shares of aggregate income using the highest quintile, $57,957 per year and higher.Actual data was rounded to whole numbers. Total may not equal 100%.

What Holds People Back?

In our practice, we engage in many consultations with prospective clients. During the consultations, we notice various common refrains from individuals. No matter the net worth or income, most people feel as if they don't have enough money and fear they will outlive their savings.

These are common fears expressed by individuals in all tax brackets, within every vocation and at all education levels. It seems that one of the most common fears among all of us is not having enough money—now and later.

There are many factors that add to this anxiety, but typically not having a plan—or not understanding the current plan is a root cause.

If you have life goals, such as a worry-free retirement, education for your children at the best schools and colleges, buying a house or a car—then building a wealth management plan can help you achieve these goals. Your plan will work towards achieving goals such as planning for your retirement, children's education, marriage, buying a house, debt management and insurance.

Wealth management planning will help you:

- categorize your risk appetite

- put a number to your goals (what is achievable and what looks difficult)

- map your current and future cash flows to your financial goals

- map your existing assets to your financial goals

- make a statement of your net worth

- look at the adequacy of your insurance

- shield your assets from potential lawsuits

- reduce taxes where possible today, potentially further increasing saving

- employ "tax diversification" techniques

- help you build a fund for your retirement

- make recommendations for your portfolio

Don't Let *Perfect* Be the Enemy of the *Good Enough*

One of the reasons some people never create a plan—or continue to engage in a planning process; is that they experience "paralysis by analysis." They decide they need a *perfect plan*, which contemplates all variables and contingencies exactly. Think about that idea for a second—how often have you tried something new, with limited knowledge on the subject matter and perfected your execution—without any help—the first time out? Probably never.

Many people will start the process only to become overloaded with ideas and scenarios. Once burdened with so much information and complexities—they shut down and never reengage.

Here is a simple, unequivocal truth: there is no perfect plan. There is no perfect plan for everyone. There is no perfect plan for you.

Even if you spend time educating yourself. Even if you hire the best expert advisors. Your plan is not going to be perfect. Even if you stumble onto the perfect plan—it will not be perfect for long, because life happens and changes will be necessary to your seemingly perfect plan.

With the burden of creating a perfect plan lifted—you now have something to work with. A good plan, is more often than not, enough. A good plan will beat having no plan...or not implementing a plan because you're trying to perfect the plan. Get started.

Why Are There No Perfect Plans?

Financial markets operate in a world of uncertainty. An experienced professional can help you recognize the series of events that are most likely to transpire. An advisor can utilize sophisticated modeling based upon a combination of current events and historical data. The reality is your goals are going to change.

Consider your priorities at age 25. It is highly likely your view of what would be important to you at age 40, is different from your way of thinking before. Experienced advisors recognize the shift in one's personal viewpoints and that the investor's aspirations are going to change. The role of a planner is to maintain ongoing dialogue and properly adjust for lifestyle changes. You need to begin saving, and allow the planner to identify appropriate investments and account registrations to meet your evolving goals.

Let's take a moment to review some of the factors that can change. These factors contribute to the paralysis experienced by many, which ultimately prevent an investor from progressing in the planning process:

- **Goals**—most people recognize the need to save for retirement. As we showed above, defined benefit plans (pension plans) are not nearly as common today as they were in the 1970s and 80s. Employees are living longer in retirement and corporations are shifting the burden of saving for retirement onto employees via defined contribution plans (401ks and 403bs). The future of entitlement programs like social security has come into question with the evolving demographic trends in the United States. Investors have recognized this trend, and have generally made saving for retirement a priority. Confusion sets in when shorter term goals must be weighed against the need to fund retirement. These goals can range from purchasing a home, funding a child's education, assisting aging parents, or maintaining support for adult children. Each of the previously mentioned shorter term needs can divert funds from the initial goal of maximizing retirement funding. How does one allocate assets appropriately to find the proper balance to achieve these goals?

- **Investment Returns**—Generally, this book has demonstrated that markets are unpredictable and market timing is essentially impossible—especially done to generate higher market returns. Rather we espouse the utilization of a long-term strategy that works with your risk profile and financial goals—with less focus on short-term returns.

- **Inflation**—this term effectively describes erosion in purchasing power. Simply put, a dollar in 1980 was worth more than a dollar today. Prices of goods and services have historically increased at a rate of slightly over 3 percent per year. Translation: prices tend to double every 20 years. In 1980 inflation exceeded 13 percent, while in 2009 the United States experienced deflation (a drop in average prices). How does one take this information and utilize this data to develop a sound wealth management plan? An investment strategy that is too conservative will experience an erosion of purchasing power, and the investor could even an experience a negative real return once accounting for inflation and taxes. Stocks have traditionally served as a preferred hedge against inflation. Why do stocks typically thrive in an inflationary environment? Corporations traditionally pass increased costs to consumers, increasing cash flow, raising dividends, maintaining profit growth, and ultimately expanding operations. Hyper-inflation can certainly create an unfavorable environment for equities; however, a moderate amount of inflation is typically positive for stocks. How do you create the appropriate mix of assets to allow you to meet your desired goals?

- **Income**—numerous unforeseen factors can impact future income, both positively and negatively. Have you left an employer and started your own business/practice? Has industry consolidation required your company to merge, altering the terms of your contract? You may experience a gradual or sudden increase in compensation. The standard of living you have today may very well be much different than your lifestyle in a decade. Retirement income needs may increase proportionally with an increase in compensation, therefore allocating additional funds to support several decades of retirement spending is imperative. An experienced planner will assist you in developing a strategy for your changes in lifestyle.

- **Saving Rate**—as compensation increases, discretionary income is certainly going to escalate. While saving more than 10 percent of your income may be challenging at age 25, this may not be the case at age 45. Annual conversations with a planner will allow you to adjust your plan favorably, potentially allowing for an early retirement.

- **Taxes**—our country has a progressive tax system. A byproduct of an increase in income is an escalating tax liability. Taking advantage of tax favored investment strategies becomes of greater importance as one's tax rate rises. Utilizing 401(k)s, Roth conversions, municipal bonds, exchange traded funds, and cash value life insurance, allows an affluent investor to create a tax-efficient retirement portfolio. Most investors recognize tax diversification is an important strategy in one's accumulation phase of planning (we discuss how this helps with planning flexibility further below). Self-directed investors often fail to develop a tax-efficient distribution strategy. A corporate executive or other investor in the highest tax bracket may accumulate $3 million in a tax deferred account. The reality is that if the same investor remains in the highest tax bracket at retirement, roughly half of the funds will be used to pay taxes. Our nation's top tax rate has changed considerably over the last century, and predicting that rate 30 years from now can be an act in futility. In 1915, the top marginal federal tax rate was 7 percent. High earners experienced a top rate of 50 percent in 1986, while a rate of 91 percent in 1963 make today's top federal rate of 39.6 percent appear to be a bargain! Tax planning will continue to be a challenge for investors as our country faces an aging population and the burden of a heavy debt load driven by escalating costs of entitlement programs. An effective wealth management plan includes a flexible and evolving tax strategy.

Elements of a Comprehensive Wealth Management Plan

Waiting for a perfect plan will put you behind. Do not use this as another excuse not to get started. The elements of your plan may differ from someone else's plan. In fact, more often than not, your specific circumstances (age, income, goals, etc.) will dictate which elements should be emphasized.

A sound plan involves more than saving, investing, and rebalancing. If you want a plan that is truly comprehensive, you want to consider additional sophisticated strategies as you begin to accumulate wealth.

The elements of a sound wealth management plan should generally include, at a minimum:

1. Investment Planning

2. Asset Protection Planning

3. Tax Planning

4. Insurance Planning

5. Education Planning

6. Financial Modeling/Retirement Projections

7. Estate Planning

8. Flexibility

Each of the above elements has their own technical aspects that can be competently handled by an advisor who has expertise in that area. Although it is common to find an advisor who has expertise in several areas, there are categories in which the input of two or more advisors may be necessary. For example, tax issues are typically handled by a both a tax attorney and a CPA. As a result, there is no way that a small team of one or two advisors could possibly handle the needs of a client. As mentioned before, this means that an individual may need to leverage the services of six or more advisors over the course of their planning lifetime.

Depending on your circumstances, planning can get complicated. There are many moving parts and the process necessitates gathering documents and statements from many different places. The best advisors know their strengths. For now, consider the following questions in each category:

1. Investment Planning
In a nutshell, the investment portion of your plan should be able to answer questions like these:

- What are you seeking to achieve for you and your family; future generations?

- What is your most important objective?

- What is your timeframe for achieving these goals?

- What do you feel is the most pressing issue related to your current portfolio?

- Describe your investment strategy?

- Who generates investment decisions?

- What process do you employ to select the makeup of your portfolio?

- What factors have you taken into consideration when structuring your portfolio for tax efficiency?

- How does your current provider work with your accountant to minimize your tax liability?

- What is your process for rebalancing the portfolio?

If you are unsure of the answer to any of the questions above, talk to your advisor—or start talking to an advisor as soon as possible.

2. Asset Protection

 This is an area which happens to be fairly specialized and is extremely important for high net worth individuals, especially those in the highest-exposure careers. Many planners are not comfortable discussing this topic with their clients. Your advisor should have a basic understanding of the risks associated with your profession, and the core strategies that can be implemented to minimize your liability to frivolous lawsuits. We are living in litigious times, and as your wealth increases, the odds of facing a suit become increasingly likely. Are you using the proper account registration to hold your assets? Did you realize some states offer substantially better asset protection than others? Are you aware you can establish an entity, such as a family limited partnership, limited liability company, or even trust in a state which you do not reside? Do you understand the difference between Joint Tenants with Rights of Survivorship, and Tenancy By Entirety? Your planner should have a basic understanding of these strategies, and be comfortable introducing you to counsel that can design strategies to protect your wealth from those who may be a threat to your nest egg.

- Have you had an asset protection analysis?

- Do you understand the relative costs/benefits or

various tools available to you?

- Have legal, insurance, and exempt tools been explained to you?

- Is your plan/analysis inclusive of both business and personal assets?

3. Tax Planning

Tax planning is an area that can demonstrate immediate value. Tax planning is simply using legitimate and legal approaches to pay less in taxes. Tax planning is not tax avoidance. Tax planning is looking at all taxes—federal, state and local income, property and capital gains—and seeing how accounting for all of them can affect your actual returns and savings. Tax planning is answering questions like:

- Has another tax expert reviewed your tax returns to give you a second opinion?

- Do you currently have a tax-loss harvesting strategy in your investment plan?

- Do you have a gifting strategy in place for appreciated assets?

- Are you using a tax-maximized qualified plan? Non-qualified plan

- Is tax diversification part of your long-term wealth management plan?

Your investment accounts are treated differently depending on what type of accounts you have. Tax planning ensures that you account for how each of your investments will be taxed—such as, using tax-deferred and tax-advantaged accounts versus taxable accounts.

As your income goes up, your eligibility for many credits and deductions goes down. A worthwhile advisor should be helping you navigate the tax consequences of all your financial decisions. Your advisor should help you monitor your tax burden to ensure it is not more onerous than necessary.

You are required to pay taxes, but you are not obligated to pay more than your fair share—nobody is bound to choose to pay more than necessary and there is nothing wrong with planning and arranging your wealth management plan to keep your taxes as low as possible under the current rules and regulations.

4. Insurance Planning

Have you adequately prepared for an unforeseen event? If you are currently in your first 10-15 years of your career, your greatest asset may very well be your future earning power. A disability policy can protect you against an illness or injury that could potentially take away your future income stream. A life insurance policy can protect your family in the event the unthinkable occurs, an untimely passing.

Cash value insurance may provide the opportunity to accumulate assets tax free, and if properly structured, can provide a tax-free source of income in your retirement years. Life insurance has often been associated with negative stereotypes, in many cases it is not properly understood by the individual selling the policy. When utilized properly, insurance can become a vital wealth management planning tool to accumulate wealth and protect your family against catastrophic events. Business owners commonly use insurance as critical component of a buy/sell exit strategy. Insurance can be used as a wealth transfer strategy, or as a method to help cover an estate tax liability. Ask your planner about the insurance policies that are most suitable for your particular situation.

- What was your intent when purchasing your insurance policy?

- Who are named as the beneficiaries?

- When what the last time you looked at your coverage to determine if it is adequate?

- Given what has happened in the financial markets in recent years, how has your current provider worked with you to make certain you have appropriate coverage?

- How often do you and your current provider review your current insurance policies?

5. Education Planning

What does it mean to you and your family to cover education costs? Fully, partially, state university or private? Do you plan to use cash flow to cover some of the costs of education? Do you understand all of the credits available in the current tax code? What is the strategy to combine savings, cash flow, scholarships and taxes for education?

- With education costs typically rising approximately 8 percent per year, how do you plan to help fund your child/children's education?

- What (if any) planning have you done to plan for your children's education?

6. Financial Modeling/Retirement Projections

At is basic level—financial modeling is using standard formulas to help plan for retirement (or another large financial goal). We use financial modeling to answer the basic questions:

- When will I be able to retire?

- How much will I need to retire—and maintain the standard of living I am accustomed to?

- How will changes in tax rates affect my plans?

- What would happen if I got sick/disabled and could no longer work?

- What happens if I live past 80 or 90 years?

Financial Modeling is not a 'one-size fits all', static exercise; it is unique and dynamic to each individual or family. Financial modeling/planning is not something that you perform once and then ignore until you retire. Your financial model must be flexible enough to evolve with you and your family, or you and your business—but the model should be able enough to guide you during a short-term crisis.

There are so many aspects that go into a wealth management plan—having even one assumption or input change can drastically impact your ability to reach your goal(s). We constantly stress the importance of having a good wealth management plan, however, also acknowledge the limitations. Most of the limitations are rooted in the many assumptions that one will need to make to arrive at an output. Assumptions such as inflation rates, tax rates, rates of return, annual investment contributions, age of retirement, longevity age, and so on.

Most individuals may approach the 'equation' in different ways; we position wealth management planning as being more of an art than a science. Many individuals will choose to view wealth management planning from a worst-case scenario perspective so they feel prepared for the many 'what ifs' that can occur. This allows you to create an action plan should those extreme scenarios play out in real time.

7. Estate Planning

 You do not necessarily need to be wealthy to begin estate planning. Everyone should have four basic estate planning documents —A basic will, durable power of attorney, medical power of attorney, and a living will. In some states, a living trust (also called revocable family trust) is standard. Individuals with a large net worth can consider any number of trusts—from GRATs, to SLATS to CLTs and CRTs and more. These documents provide a variety of benefits beyond the scope of this Lesson. Ask your planner which of these strategies are most appropriate for you and your family. Your planner should have relationships with local attorneys familiar with these concepts who understand state laws, which can vary drastically in various parts of the country.

- When was the last time you reviewed your estate plan?

- How often do you review your plan to make certain it is still appropriate for your circumstances?

- What are you seeking to accomplish with the plan you currently have in place?

- Should something happen to you and your spouse, how will your minor children be provided for?

- How have you structured your plan to minimize/eliminate unnecessary taxes?

These are the topics you should be thinking about when putting together your plan—or when reviewing your current plan. These are the questions your advisor should be asking you. These are the fact finding, data gathering questions of a true fiduciary looking to partner with you on creating a wealth management plan. These are not questions of a salesperson looking to sell you the latest investment product.

8. Flexibility: A Crucial Success Factor in Any Plan

So much of life doesn't work out exactly as we expect. As such, it is obvious that flexibility should be fundamental to your wealth management plan. Many factors that may make the difference between hitting your financial goals or not are beyond your control.

Changes in income (or cash flow); changes in tax rates; market changes; potential changes in liability and your personal health can all severely hinder you from reaching your goals—let's take a quick look at each:

- **Changes in income and cash flow:** are important to consider in any wealth management plan. The fact is most investors cannot accurately predict their income in future years right now, so flexibility must be part of their plan.

How do you incorporate income/cash flow flexibility into a plan? By living below your means and prioritizing saving each month, quarter and year. These two elements may combine to position you to weather any temporary or even long-term hits to income/cash flow.

Another tactic could be implementation of a savings vehicle that allows for uneven funding/investments. As an example, in the qualified retirement plan (QRP) arena, this might mean using defined contribution plans that allow flexibility in contributions each year, as opposed to a defined benefit plan which can require a certain level of funding or cause underfunding penalties. Even more relevant would be to utilize non-qualified plans that may allow much higher contributions than defined contribution plans when income is high, but can actually be skipped entirely in years where income wanes.

Another example here would be in the asset class of permanent life insurance, one that has the benefit of tax-deferred growth and top asset protection in many states. Here, funding flexibility would favor a "universal life" policy, where funding is flexible year-to-year, over a "whole life" policy, where funding must occur each year.

- **Changes in Tax Rates:** Since 2013, when the rates last changed, many business owners and high net worth individuals now pay a top marginal tax rate of over 50 percent, when federal and state incomes taxes, as well as self-employment taxes are considered. This doesn't include local income, property or sales taxes. With a new administration in the White House since early 2017, rates may change.

  Still, until rates change once again, we are at

the fourth lowest federal income tax regime (measured by the highest bracket) since the income tax was implemented just over 100 years ago, and the second lowest capital gains tax rates since the 1940s when that tax was enacted. See the charts below, which show the top marginal federal income tax rate and federal capital gains tax rate in effect for each decade on the "0 year" (i.e., 1920, 1930, 1940, 1950, etc.). These charts do not show state income or capital gains rates.

Top Federal Income Tax Rates

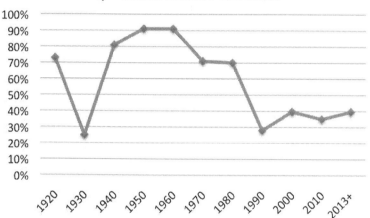

Source: Citizens for Tax Justice

Federal Capital Gains Tax Rate

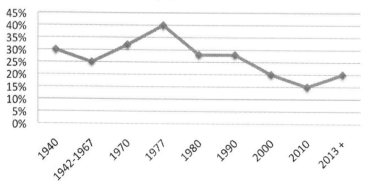

Source: Citizens for Tax Justice

Examining these charts, it seems quite possible that we could see tax rates continue to rise even more over the long term, regardless of short-term changes that might be made in the next four to eight years. If they even return to mean rates of the 20th century, we will experience a sharp increase in tax rates. Thus, it makes sense to build in flexibility for this possibility.

A "tax diversification" approach can help alleviate some potential issues. While most plans focus only on asset class diversification in the context of investing, we believe it is crucial to layer on top of this focus a concentration to diversify your wealth to tax rate exposure.

Applying a "diversification" approach generally sheds light on the fact that most investors with some type of plan are still inadequately invested in asset classes or structures that are immune to future income or capital gains tax increases. Whether these options are in the form of cash value life insurance, tax-free municipal bonds, Roth IRAs or others, they should be part of many wealth-building plans. Bottom line: you need to have flexibility against the possibility that tax rates increase, especially if those increases are significant.

Seemingly every new presidential administration seeks to change the Tax Code. The post-2016 tax world could look very different from the current world. As intentions come into focus and changes are (or are not) implemented—it becomes increasing important to have a flexible plan in place (and the right advisors to help keep you up-to-date and ready to pivot when necessary).

- **Changes in the "Market":** The reason we put the word "Market" in quotes is that we mean more than a small sample of the stock market in the U.S., such as the Dow 30 or even the S&P 500 indices. What we are trying to get at here is the concept that there is volatility in all of the securities, commodities, real estate and other asset marketplaces in the U.S. and all over the world. As we showed in Lessons Two; values go up and they go down in all asset classes.

Throughout the previous Lessons, we discussed that most savvy investors understand that portfolio diversification is a key consideration to reducing some of the risk of loss in a portfolio. In historically volatile markets, mitigation of loss is not a luxury, it is a necessity. Proper diversification, especially in a highly volatile market must also be across investment classes and not just within a class (such as securities or real estate). A balance of domestic and foreign securities, real estate, small businesses, commodities, and other alternative investments would prove to be much less risky than holding the majority of your investments in real estate and securities (which is what most individuals do).

- **Changes in Liability:** One of the authors of this book spent over a decade as an attorney specializing in asset protection planning. This area is important to him. What one must realize is that any planning designed to shield wealth from a lawsuit claimant, creditor, or even soon-to-be ex-spouse is typically not effective if implemented after you have notice of a claim or threat. Simply put, you must put asset protection planning in place before there is a problem.

  The challenge is that many clients want to maintain ownership of the asset, control of the asset, and access of the asset, or some combination of all three, at times where there is no liability threat lurking. Fortunately, with comprehensive asset protection planning, utilizing exempt assets, legal tools, insurances and proper ownership forms, the client's goals here can typically be accomplished.

Thus, you can generally build flexibility into your planning by using tools that shield wealth if, or when, you have liability threats, but allow you ownership, control and/or access to that wealth when "the coast is clear."

- **Changes in Your Health:** Your health is the most important element of all. At one extreme, being in good health is a blessing and can allow you to be more productive and create more wealth, as well as allow you to share it, enjoy it, and even give it away. On the other extreme, poor health can keep you from earning a living, and can even lead to premature death, which can have a devastating economic impact to the family. For these reasons, it is crucial that a conservative wealth plan build flexibility around changes in health.

  The first way to build flexibility here is to secure the proper insurances to shield your ability to earn income. There are two important insurances to examine: one that provides you a regular income stream if you become disabled and one that provides your heirs financial protection in case you die. We are, of course, describing disability insurance and life insurance.

  Certainly, if you are concerned only about your own ability to meet your financial goals and have no financial dependents, then disability insurance may be the only coverage on which to focus. The data tell us all that the likelihood that we will incur a significant long-term disability is much higher than dying prematurely. Nonetheless, in our experience, most high-earners are significantly under-insured for disability. As such, they are risking all of their financial goals on their ability to avoid disability. This is not a risk we encourage you to take.

  As for life insurance, there are many different

types of products: from term to cash value, and whole life to private placement. Whatever product you use, you need to plan around having adequate coverage given your income, debt, assets, family situation, tax rate, state of residency and goals. This is very much a case-by-case analysis based on your individual situation.

Value of Financial Specialists

For some people, managing their own wealth may appear easy; save more, spend less is a plan. It is a vague plan with little in the way of keeping track. It has no timeline and few (if any) realistic measurable benchmarks for success. There are no long-term targets to aim for. It is less a plan, and more an aspiration.

A General Practitioner is perfect for most patients—someone they can go to for general health questions and prescriptions for colds and fevers. However, as we get older, our GP may start referring us to specialists to assist and even lead on certain health conditions. Everyone recognizes the value of both generalists and specialists in the medical arena—the financial services industry is similar.

A great way best way to maximize your wealth management is by leveraging experts. This is valuable at all levels—but especially as you accumulate more wealth. As your wealth grows—so does the level of complexity involved in managing it.

Complexity generally necessitates the need for a team of advisors. Without a very strong team, you will struggle to find the time to focus on the important things that make you money, let alone enjoy any free time.

Below we discuss the reason *why* you need a team of knowledgeable advisors with diverse areas of expertise. Then we will discuss *how* to maximize the value of your advisors and suggest tips for working with your team.

Most people realize that wealth creates complexity. What you need to realize is that the management of complexity and leverage is not the job of a traffic cop. As wealth grows, the number of complicated, technical risks that an investor faces also grows exponentially.

As an example, in a business—the transition from running a sole proprietorship to having a single employee may not seem to be major, but that couldn't be further from the truth. The addition of just one employee creates a need for:

- *Payroll creation, funding, and payments*

- *Regular payroll tax payments (or you can go to jail)*

- *Withholding tax filings and payments*

- *Workers compensation insurance or fund payments*

- *Occupation Safety Hazard Association (OSHA) compliance*

- *Separate retirement plan (ERISA) regulations and contribution requirements*

- *A host of other state and federal reporting requirements*

In addition, the leverage of assets also increases the need for more general categories of planning, like asset protection, banking (private and commercial), business planning, financial planning, investing, life insurance analysis, disability insurance analysis, property and casualty insurance analysis, long-term care insurance analysis, educational funding, retirement planning, family law, gift and estate tax planning, charitable planning, and numerous other areas.

Each category of planning has its own technical areas that can be competently handled by an advisor who has expertise in that area. Although it is common to find an advisor who has expertise in several areas, there are categories in which the input of two advisors may be necessary. For example, tax issues are typically handled by both a tax attorney and a CPA.

As a result, there is no way that a small team of two or three advisors could possibly handle the needs of an investor with a more complex wealth management plan. This means that you may need to leverage the services of more advisors over your lifetime.

In these situations—it is best to pick a trusted advisor to oversee the entire plan and function as your quarterback—someone who can corral all the other advisors and keep everyone working on the same page towards your financial goals.

You may be thinking:

- I am not high net worth.

- My plan is not complex enough for multiple advisors.

- I'm just trying to get started!

All, or some this, may be true—but proactive planning requires you to start thinking about these concepts *before* they become full-fledged issues that require *immediate* attention.

Understanding the necessity of *help* is the first step—finding the *right help* is the obvious next step. Coordinating the help and advice and implementing your plan is an ongoing endeavor.

Even if you have a team of highly-experienced advisors in the fields of tax, law, insurance and investments working for you, your plan can still be in complete disarray. If the advisors are not collaborating to utilize their collective expertise to implement a comprehensive, multidisciplinary plan for your benefit, your planning will suffer significantly.

All too often, we see the symptoms of such a lack of coordination. Clients who come to our offices often have paid a technically sound attorney to create a comprehensive living trust, but the family's assets have not yet been titled to the trust (potentially making the document useless). We frequently see life insurance policies and life insurance trusts that, because the proper steps were not taken to combine the two vehicles, do not work as they should.

Like the radiologist, surgeon, and anesthesiologist who must work together to make sure a patient has a successful surgery, your CPA, attorney and financial advisors *must* work together to help you successfully achieve your financial goals. If the surgeon never saw the films or charts, or the anesthesiologist and surgeon didn't speak, it would be pretty difficult to successfully treat a surgical patient.

Building a Plan for All Stages: Dynamic and Proactive Versus Reactive

What does it mean to be *reactive*, compared to *proactive* in wealth management planning?

At its most basic level, *reactive* implies that you do not take the initiative. Rather, you let circumstances and events dictate. In contrast, the image we associate with *proactive* is one of action and preparation—setting a course and moving a specified direction with a specified purpose.

When acting in a reactive manner, we tend to wait for problems, issues and opportunities to appear—then figure out what to do. When acting in a proactive manner, we tend to consider possible problems, issues and opportunities and determine how we will handle them when they appear.

Planning is generally proactive in nature. However, crafting a plan—and failing to monitor it is at best passive/reactive. Crafting a plan and revisiting it at regular intervals or during major life changes is proactive and dynamic.

Many times, we meet with clients who are more *reactive*—meaning they make many their financial decisions based on the past and then try their best to react properly to events that have already happened.

Why is this? Because typically that is how their advice is coming to them from their current advisor: reacting to past events, thinking the future can be controlled.

Conclusion

Having a plan will not remove all financial stress from your life. Life will continue to throw curveballs and cause your plan to be adjusted. A *static-reactive* plan will give a great sense of relief or at the very least clarity generally right after completion, but if this plan is not *actively* updated and flexible, then it will provide little in the way of long-term relief of your daily financial stress.

We often tell clients that financial services are filled with advice that lacks objectivity, transparency and many times is not in your best interest. It is no wonder financial stress once again sits at the top of the rankings. Not only is it difficult to become financially independent—it can sometimes become more difficult to find advice you trust.

Like the quote leading off this Lesson states; a goal without a plan is a wish. Are you willing to stake your future on a wish? Are you prepared to leave your life up to chance? Of course not. Start your plan. Revisit your plan. Make certain you can tell if you are following your plan.

Stop putting it off. Alleviate at least some of the financial stress you feel.

What is Next?

We hope this book has helped frame wealth management in a simpler way than what you have considered in the past. Now that you have read all (or just a few) lessons, go back to the introduction and review some of the questions.

Do you feel a little more confident in responding? If not, do you at least feel a little more confident in figuring out how to find the answers? We hope so.

Do you understand your options for professional investment advice and why most individual investors get great value over time from the right advisor? Do you know how your present advisor makes money and what type of duty they owe you? Are you able to ask the right questions of an existing investment professional... or a potential one? Can you identify, and try to avoid, the common pitfalls that plague most investors?

Perhaps most importantly, do you understand the importance of a comprehensive wealth management plan for your future... and how your investments fit into that plan?

Again, we hope so.

We wrote this short book because we know that you are extremely busy.

The same is true for most investors when it comes to a high

level of planning. Even though it may produce a more efficient risk-adjusted investment portfolio, save them taxes, build them wealth for retirement, and protect what they've worked so hard to acquire, most people still never get to it.

That is why we keep our process efficient. If we can get on the phone for just 25 minutes, we can determine if we can help you with your leading wealth planning concerns—whether that is a comprehensive plan, a review of your investments or other wealth management disciplines—from asset protection planning, tax reduction, and corporate structure, to insurances, college education planning or retirement modeling. And, yes, we will be able to determine if one or more of the tools we have used for hundreds of investors across the country might work for you—to better help you reduce risk, improve returns, and get you closer to your long-term wealth management goals.

Our consultations are always complimentary, and we can speak with you during the workday, in the evening or on weekends. Please give us a call at 877-656-4362; or reach out to schedule a consultation on our website at www.ojmgroup.com.

Wealth management is not easy—but it can be simplified with education, organization and a little help. We hope this book will remain a helpful resource for you and we thank you again for taking time out of your busy schedule to read it. If nothing else, you have armed yourself with information on where to start... or how to review your current plan to determine if you are on the right track.

Remember, there is no such thing as a perfect plan—so don't wait for the perfect timing—*the best time to start is now.*

Your next steps are simple...but not easy. Good luck.

Like what you've read?

Follow us for up-to-date information on everything you've read here:

 /OJMGROUP /OJMGROUP COMPANY/OJMGROUP

Ready to act?

Whether you're looking for an advisor, or currently working with one, we would love to chat about your goals and what you thought of our book.

OJM Group is a multidisciplinary wealth management firm comprised of a team of experienced advisors with one unifying goal: helping our clients build and preserve wealth. We have worked with over 1,000 clients in 48 states and are proud of our reputation as thought leaders in our field.

We work with clients in three ways:

1. *Investment Management:* OJM manages over a quarter of a billion dollars using a client-aligned business model. Our innovative investment methods also integrate best practices in asset protection and tax minimization.

2. *Consulting:* With our unique consulting process, OJM can help clients with just one planning area, or we can become the client's *financial quarterback*, coordinating all areas of their financial life.

3. *Insurance and Benefits Planning:* In addition to our expertise in life, disability and long-term care insurance planning, OJM team members have over 70 years of collective experience in qualified and non-qualified plans.

Our initial consultation is offered at no charge and there are no obligations or strings attached. To schedule your consultation, please call 877-656-4362 or email any of the authors. Thanks for reading.

David B. Mandell, JD, MBA
mandell@ojmgroup.com

Jason M. O'Dell, MS, CWM
odell@ojmgroup.com

Carole C. Foos, CPA
carole@ojmgroup.com

SCHEDULE A SEMINAR

David, Jason, Carole and their team have presented seminars in all parts of the country on corporate structure, tax reduction, asset protection, financial planning and investing.

Please contact Guardian Publishing at 513-792-1252 to schedule a call to discuss how one of our speakers could deliver a lecture for your group or association.

www.guardpub.com

REQUEST AUTHORS' ARTICLES
FOR YOUR PUBLICATION

The authors of Guardian Publishing have written articles for over 100 periodicals, newsletters and websites. The authors have also appeared on hundreds of radio shows and on Bloomberg and Fox television.

We can provide the content to educational publications at no cost, provided the articles include bylines that instruct readers how to reach the authors if they have questions or require some consulting assistance.

If you are interested in publishing articles by the authors on asset protection, business planning, benefit planning, retirement, insurance, tax or investing, please contact Guardian Publishing at 513-792-1252.

www.guardpub.com

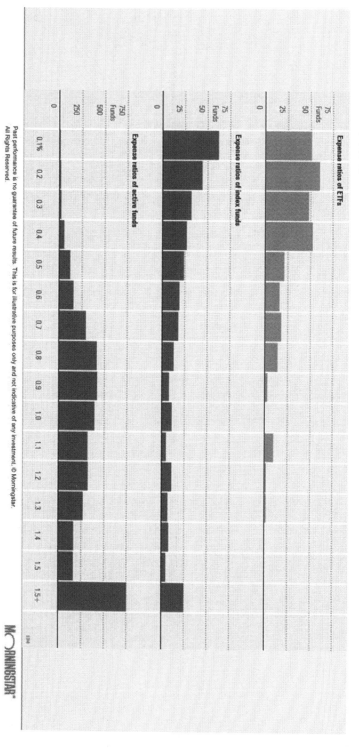

Expense Ratios of Large-Caps: ETFs, Index Funds, and Active Funds

As of December 2016

Expense ratios of ETFs

Expense ratios of index funds

Expense ratios of active funds

Magnified chart from page 11

Demonstration of Value of $1 Invested in the DOW in 1920, Bloomberg, LP

Magnified chart from page 34

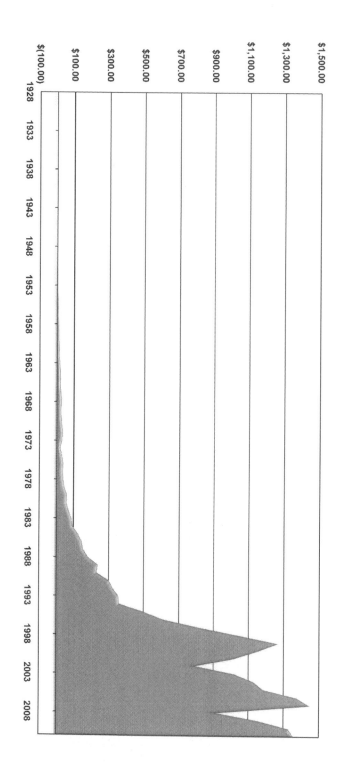

Demonstration of Value of $1 Invested in the S&P in 1928, Bloomberg, LP

Magnified chart from page 34

Asset-Class Winners and Losers 2002-2016

Rank (Best→Worst)	2002	2003	2004	2005	2006	2007	2008	2009	2010	2011	2012	2013	2014	2015	2016	15-Year Return
1	Fixed Income 10.3%	EM Stocks 55.8%	EM Stocks 25.6%	EM Stocks 34.0%	EM Stocks 32.1%	EM Stocks 39.4%	Fixed Income 5.2%	EM Stocks 78.5%	US Small Stocks 26.9%	Fixed Income 7.8%	EM Stocks 18.2%	US Small Stocks 38.8%	US Large Stocks 13.7%	US Large Stocks 1.4%	US Small Stocks 21.3%	EM Stocks 9.5%
2	EM Stocks -6.2%	US Small Stocks 47.3%	Dev Intl Stocks 20.2%	Dev Intl Stocks 13.5%	Dev Intl Stocks 26.3%	Dev Intl Stocks 11.7%	Balanced Portfolio -22.8%	Dev Intl Stocks 34.6%	EM Stocks 18.9%	US Large Stocks 2.1%	Dev Intl Stocks 17.3%	US Large Stocks 32.4%	Fixed Income 6.0%	Fixed Income 0.5%	US Large Stocks 12.0%	US Small Stocks 8.5%
3	Balanced Portfolio -9.4%	Dev Intl Stocks 38.6%	US Small Stocks 18.3%	Global Stocks 10.8%	Global Stocks 21.0%	Global Stocks 11.2%	US Small Stocks -33.8%	US Small Stocks 31.8%	US Large Stocks 15.1%	Balanced Portfolio 1.9%	US Small Stocks 16.3%	Global Stocks 22.8%	Balanced Portfolio 6.0%	Balanced Portfolio -0.8%	EM Stocks 11.2%	US Large Stocks 6.7%
4	Dev Intl Stocks -15.9%	Global Stocks 34.0%	Global Stocks 15.2%	Balanced Portfolio 5.2%	US Small Stocks 18.4%	Fixed Income 7.0%	US Large Stocks -37.0%	US Large Stocks 27.2%	Global Stocks 12.7%	US Small Stocks -4.2%	Global Stocks 16.1%	Dev Intl Stocks 22.8%	US Small Stocks 4.9%	Dev Intl Stocks -1.5%	Balanced Portfolio 7.9%	Global Stocks 5.9%
5	Global Stocks -19.3%	US Large Stocks 28.7%	US Large Stocks 10.9%	US Large Stocks 4.9%	US Large Stocks 15.8%	Balanced Portfolio 6.8%	Global Stocks -42.2%	Global Stocks 26.5%	Balanced Portfolio 12.6%	Global Stocks -7.3%	US Large Stocks 16.0%	Balanced Portfolio 12.1%	Global Stocks 4.2%	Global Stocks -2.4%	Global Stocks 7.8%	Balanced Portfolio 5.7%
6	US Small Stocks -20.5%	Balanced Portfolio 21.0%	Balanced Portfolio 9.9%	US Small Stocks 4.6%	Balanced Portfolio 12.5%	US Large Stocks 5.5%	Dev Intl Stocks -43.4%	Balanced Portfolio 19.9%	Dev Intl Stocks 7.8%	Dev Intl Stocks -12.1%	Balanced Portfolio 12.1%	Fixed Income -2.0%	EM Stocks -2.2%	US Small Stocks -4.4%	Fixed Income 2.6%	Dev Intl Stocks 5.3%
7	US Large Stocks -22.1%	Fixed Income 4.1%	Fixed Income 4.3%	Fixed Income 2.4%	Fixed Income 4.3%	US Small Stocks -1.6%	EM Stocks -53.3%	Fixed Income 5.9%	Fixed Income 6.5%	EM Stocks -18.4%	Fixed Income 4.2%	EM Stocks -2.6%	Dev Intl Stocks -4.9%	EM Stocks -14.9%	Dev Intl Stocks 1.0%	Fixed Income 4.6%

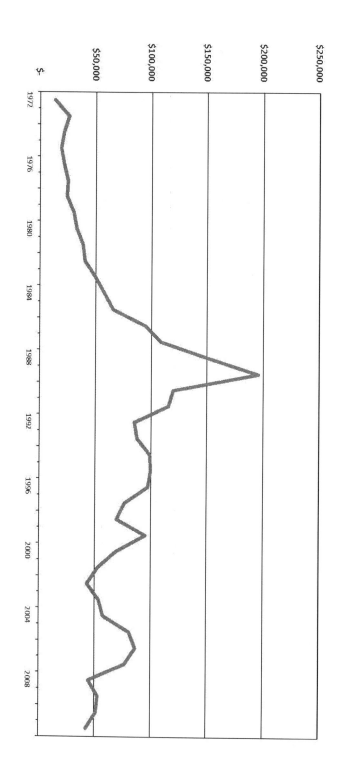

NIKKEI from 1970 through 2011: Bloomberg, LP

Magnified chart from page 44

NIKKEI Returns 1991-2010. Source: Bloomberg, LP

Magnified chart from page 45

Asset-Class Winners and Losers 2002-2016

Worst ← ————————————————————— → Best

Rank	2002	2003	2004	2005	2006	2007	2008	2009	2010	2011	2012	2013	2014	2015	2016	15-Year Return
Best	Fixed Income 10.3%	EM Stocks 55.8%	EM Stocks 25.6%	EM Stocks 34.0%	EM Stocks 32.1%	EM Stocks 39.4%	Fixed Income 5.2%	EM Stocks 78.5%	US Small Stocks 26.9%	Fixed Income 7.8%	EM Stocks 18.2%	US Small Stocks 38.8%	US Large Stocks 13.7%	US Large Stocks 1.4%	US Small Stocks 21.3%	EM Stocks 9.5%
	EM Stocks -6.2%	US Small Stocks 47.3%	Dev Intl Stocks 20.2%	Dev Intl Stocks 13.5%	Dev Intl Stocks 26.3%	Dev Intl Stocks 11.7%	Balanced Portfolio -22.8%	Dev Intl Stocks 34.6%	EM Stocks 18.9%	US Large Stocks 2.1%	Dev Intl Stocks 17.3%	US Large Stocks 32.4%	Balanced Portfolio 6.0%	Fixed Income 0.5%	US Large Stocks 12.0%	US Small Stocks 8.5%
	Balanced Portfolio -9.4%	Dev Intl Stocks 38.6%	US Small Stocks 18.3%	Global Stocks 10.8%	Global Stocks 21.0%	Global Stocks 11.2%	US Small Stocks -33.8%	Global Stocks 31.8%	US Large Stocks 15.1%	Balanced Portfolio 1.9%	US Small Stocks 16.3%	Dev Intl Stocks 22.8%	Fixed Income 6.0%	Dev Intl Stocks -0.8%	EM Stocks 11.2%	US Large Stocks 6.7%
	Dev Intl Stocks -15.9%	Global Stocks 34.0%	Global Stocks 15.2%	Balanced Portfolio 5.2%	US Small Stocks 18.4%	Fixed Income 7.0%	US Large Stocks -37.0%	US Small Stocks 27.2%	Global Stocks 12.7%	US Small Stocks -4.2%	Global Stocks 16.1%	Global Stocks 22.8%	US Small Stocks 4.9%	Balanced Portfolio -1.5%	Global Stocks 7.9%	Global Stocks 5.9%
	Global Stocks -19.3%	US Large Stocks 28.7%	US Large Stocks 10.9%	US Large Stocks 4.9%	US Large Stocks 15.8%	Balanced Portfolio 6.8%	Global Stocks -42.2%	US Large Stocks 26.5%	Balanced Portfolio 12.6%	Global Stocks -7.3%	US Large Stocks 16.0%	Balanced Portfolio 12.1%	Global Stocks 4.2%	Global Stocks -2.4%	Balanced Portfolio 7.8%	Dev Intl Stocks 5.7%
	US Small Stocks -20.5%	Balanced Portfolio 21.0%	Balanced Portfolio 9.9%	US Small Stocks 4.6%	Balanced Portfolio 12.5%	US Large Stocks 5.5%	Dev Intl Stocks -43.4%	Balanced Portfolio 19.9%	Dev Intl Stocks 7.8%	Dev Intl Stocks -12.1%	Balanced Portfolio 12.1%	Fixed Income -2.0%	EM Stocks -2.2%	US Small Stocks -4.4%	Fixed Income 2.6%	Balanced Portfolio 5.3%
Worst	US Large Stocks -22.1%	Fixed Income 4.1%	Fixed Income 4.3%	Fixed Income 2.4%	Fixed Income 4.3%	US Small Stocks -1.6%	EM Stocks -53.3%	Fixed Income 5.9%	Fixed Income 6.5%	EM Stocks -18.4%	Fixed Income 4.2%	EM Stocks -2.6%	Dev Intl Stocks -4.9%	EM Stocks -14.9%	Dev Intl Stocks 1.0%	Fixed Income 4.6%

Magnified chart from page 91

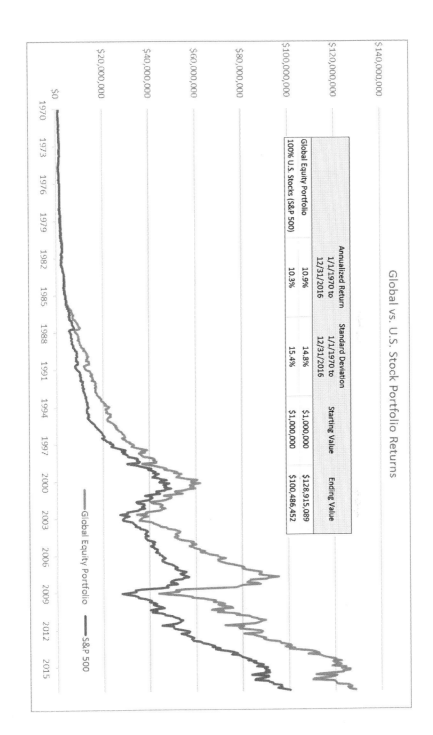

Global vs. U.S. Stock Portfolio Returns

	Annualized Return 1/1/1970 to 12/31/2016	Standard Deviation 1/1/1970 to 12/31/2016	Starting Value	Ending Value
Global Equity Portfolio	10.9%	14.8%	$1,000,000	$128,915,089
100% U.S. Stocks (S&P 500)	10.3%	15.4%	$1,000,000	$100,486,452

Global Equity Portfolio ——— S&P 500

Magnified chart from page 92

Asset Class	Global 2014	Global 2015	Global 2016	North America	Asia-Pacific (excl. Japan)	Japan	Europe	Latin America	Middle East & Africa
Alternative Investments	13.50%	13.00%	15.70%	16.00%	16.60%	14.30%	15.00%	18.90%	17.10%
Fixed Income	16.40%	16.90%	18.00%	19.60%	19.00%	13.60%	18.10%	20.30%	17.90%
Real Estate	18.70%	17.60%	17.90%	15.10%	20.50%	13.40%	21.80%	21.90%	19.80%
Cash and Cash Equivalents	26.60%	25.60%	23.50%	22.20%	20.60%	34.00%	19.90%	21.70%	26.30%
Equities	24.80%	26.80%	24.80%	27.10%	23.30%	24.70%	25.20%	17.10%	18.90%

Legend: Alternative Investments · Fixed Income · Real Estate · Cash and Cash Equivalents · Equities

Magnified chart from page 93

Hypothetical example

Year	PORTFOLIO A		PORTFOLIO B	
	Return	Balance	Return	Balance
0		$100,000		$100,000
1	−15%	$80,750	22%	$115,900
2	−4%	$72,720	8%	$119,772
3	−10%	$60,948	30%	$149,204
4	8%	$60,424	7%	$154,298
5	12%	$62,075	18%	$176,171
6	10%	$62,782	9%	$186,577
7	−7%	$53,737	28%	$232,418
8	4%	$50,687	14%	$259,257
9	−12%	$40,204	−9%	$231,374
10	13%	$39,781	16%	$262,594
11	7%	$37,216	−6%	$242,138
12	−10%	$28,994	17%	$277,452
13	19%	$28,553	19%	$324,217
14	17%	$27,557	−10%	$287,296
15	−6%	$21,204	7%	$302,056
16	16%	$18,796	13%	$335,674
17	−9%	$12,555	−12%	$290,993
18	14%	$8,612	4%	$297,433
19	28%	$4,624	−7%	$271,962
20	9%	$0	16%	$293,658
21	18%	$0	12%	$323,297
22	7%	$0	8%	$343,761
23	30%	$0	−10%	$304,885
24	8%	$0	−4%	$287,890
25	22%	$0	−15%	$240,456
Arithmetic Mean	8.8%		8.8%	
Standard Deviation	12.8%		12.8%	
Compound Growth Rate	6%		6%	

Magnified chart from page 94

The Importance of Staying Invested
Ending wealth values after a market decline

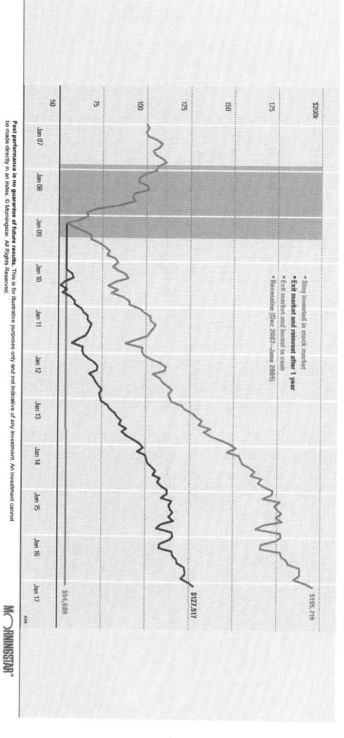

- Stay invested in stock market
- Exit market and reinvest after 1 year
- Exit market and invest in cash
- Recession (Dec 2007–June 2009)

$195,718

$127,517

$54,689

$200k

175

150

125

100

75

50

Jan 07 Jan 08 Jan 09 Jan 10 Jan 11 Jan 12 Jan 13 Jan 14 Jan 15 Jan 16 Jan 17

Past performance is no guarantee of future results. This is for illustrative purposes only and not indicative of any investment. An investment cannot be made directly in an index. © Morningstar. All Rights Reserved.

MORNINGSTAR®

Magnified chart from page 119

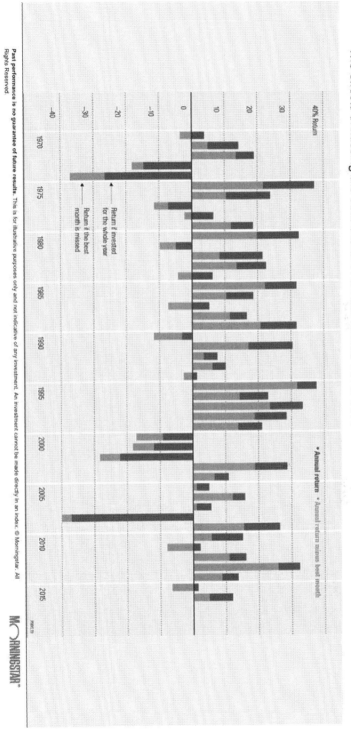

Market-Timing Risk

The effects of missing the best month of annual returns 1970–2016

- Annual return • Annual return minus best month

Return if invested
for the whole year

Return if the best
month is missed

Magnified chart from page 120

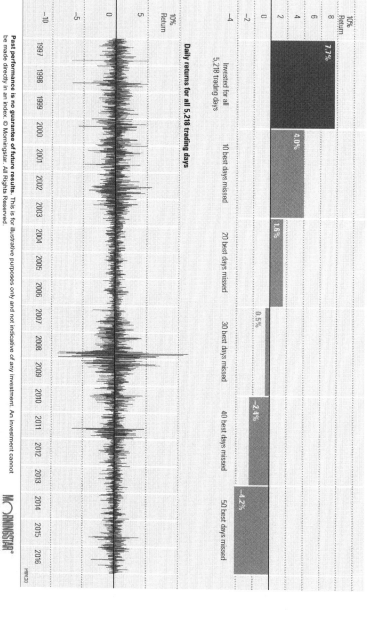

The Cost of Market Timing

Risk of missing the best days in the market 1997–2016

	Return
Invested for all 5,218 trading days	7.7%
10 best days missed	4.0%
20 best days missed	1.6%
30 best days missed	0.5%
40 best days missed	−2.4%
50 best days missed	−4.2%

Daily returns for all 5,218 trading days

MORNINGSTAR®

Magnified chart from page 121

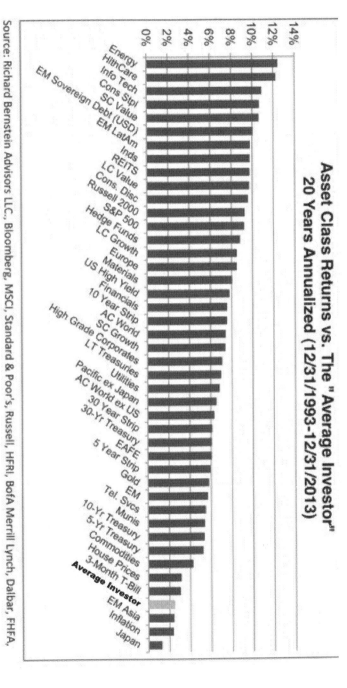

Asset Class Returns vs. The "Average Investor"
20 Years Annualized (12/31/1993-12/31/2013)

Energy
HlthCare
Info Tech
Cons Stpl
SC Value
EM Sovereign Debt (USD)
EM LatAm
Inds
REITS
LC Value
Cons. Disc
Russell 2000
S&P 500
Hedge Funds
LC Growth
Europe
Materials
US High Yield
Financials
10 Year Strip
AC Wond
SC Growth
High Grade Corporates
LT Treasuries
Utilities
Pacific ex Japan
AC World ex US
30 Year Strip
30-Yr Treasury
EAFE
5 Year Strip
Gold
EM
Tel. Svcs
Munis
10-Yr Treasury
5-Yr Treasury
Commodities
House Prices
3-Month T-Bill
Average Investor
EM Asia
Inflation
Japan

0% 2% 4% 6% 8% 10% 12% 14%

Source: Richard Bernstein Advisors LLC., Bloomberg, MSCI, Standard & Poor's, Russell, HFRI, BofA Merrill Lynch, Dalbar, FHFA, FRB, FTSE. Total Returns in USD.

Average Investor is represented by Dalbar's average asset allocation investor return, which utilizes the net of aggregate mutual fund sales, redemptions and exchanges each month as a measure of investor behavior.

For index descriptors, see "Index Descriptions" at end of document.

Magnified chart from page 122

Made in the USA
Columbia, SC
11 January 2020